C++ for Game Development & Performance

Unlock Speed, Power, and Professional Tools for High-End Applications

I0011265

Booker Blunt

Rafael Sanders

Miguel Farmer

Boozman Richard

How to Scan a Barcode to Get a Repository

1. **Install a QR/Barcode Scanner** – Ensure you have a barcode or QR code scanner app installed on your smartphone or use a built-in scanner in **GitHub, GitLab, or Bitbucket.**

2. **Open the Scanner** – Launch the scanner app and grant necessary camera permissions.

3. **Scan the Barcode** – Align the barcode within the scanning frame. The scanner will automatically detect and process it.

4. **Follow the Link** – The scanned result will display a **URL to the repository**. Tap the link to open it in your web browser or Git client.

5. **Clone the Repository** – Use **Git clone** with the provided URL to download the repository to your local machine.

Chapter 1: Introduction to C++ for Game Development

Why C++? Understanding its Importance in Game Development

Welcome to the exciting world of game development, where imagination meets code to create incredible, interactive experiences. The foundation of many of the most successful and well-known games is built on **C++**, a powerful and versatile programming language. If you're wondering why C++ is so widely used in game development, you're in the right place.

Let's start by understanding **why C++ stands out** as the language of choice for game developers.

C++: Power and Performance

Game development is inherently complex, and performance is **critical**. From graphics rendering to game physics, artificial intelligence (AI), and real-time responsiveness, every second counts. **C++** shines in these performance-heavy tasks, offering the **speed and control** that is needed for both large-scale AAA games and smaller indie projects.

The reason behind C++'s performance lies in its ability to interact directly with the system hardware, giving you low-level control over memory management and processing. Unlike higher-level languages (like Python or JavaScript), which abstract away much of this control, C++ lets developers optimize every part of their code to achieve high performance, making it ideal for **high-demand applications** like games.

Industry Adoption: From AAA Titles to Indie Games

When you look at the **big names in the gaming industry,** you'll see that **C++** is the backbone of some of the **largest and most successful games** ever made. Game engines like **Unreal Engine, CryEngine,** and **Unity (partially)** use C++ as a core language. Many **AAA games**—those multi-million dollar blockbuster titles—rely on C++ for critical systems like game rendering, physics simulation, and real-time interactions.

But it doesn't stop at AAA games. Many **indie developers** have embraced C++ for its flexibility and performance. C++ is also at the heart of popular open-source game engines like **Godot,** which gives smaller teams the power to create robust, high-performance games with fewer resources.

The Real-World Relevance of C++

While many other languages are used in game development (like C#, Java, or Python), C++ remains the **industry standard**. It's used not just in gaming but in **simulation software, real-time systems,** and **high-frequency trading platforms**—environments that require speed, reliability, and efficiency.

Now that we've touched on why C++ is so important for game development, let's compare it to other languages and see why it continues to lead in performance-heavy applications like games.

C++ vs Other Programming Languages: Why C++ Stands Out

C++ vs C#: Both C++ and C# are used in game development, but they differ in their approach. C# is more commonly associated with Unity, an engine used widely in the gaming world. While C# is easy to learn and has a cleaner syntax, C++ offers more direct control over hardware, which is important for optimizing performance.

Example: Imagine you're working on a complex physics simulation. With C++, you have **direct access to memory and processor resources**, allowing you to optimize the physics calculations in a way that's not possible with C#. While C# can be more **beginner-friendly**, C++ will give you better **control** over resource-intensive tasks.

C++ vs JavaScript: JavaScript is often used for web-based games or mobile game development. It's great for rapid development but doesn't have the performance required for high-end games. C++ on the other hand can handle high-performance graphics and intensive computation that JavaScript struggles with.

Example: JavaScript can create fun, browser-based games like puzzle games or card games, but when you need to simulate realistic 3D physics for a first-person shooter, C++ is the **go-to language**.

C++ vs Python: Python is incredibly popular for scripting, AI, and game prototyping due to its simplicity and ease of use. However, when it comes to final game production, C++ excels because of its low-level access to system hardware.

Example: Python may be used to **script AI behaviors** or manage resources during early development stages. But once the game is moving towards finalization, C++ is often required to make sure it runs smoothly and efficiently.

C++: The Best of Both Worlds

C++ allows you to write **high-level code** (for easy interaction) and **low-level code** (for optimization and control). This **flexibility** makes it stand out in game development because it gives developers a **broad range of tools** to work with, from **simple scripting** to **complex performance tweaks**.

Setting Up Your Development Environment

Now that we've understood the "why" behind using C++ in game development, let's move on to setting up your environment.

What You'll Need: Software and Hardware Suggestions

Before jumping into coding, we need to get your environment set up. Here's what you'll need:

- **Software:**

  - **IDE (Integrated Development Environment):** This is where you'll write your code. The two most popular options are:

    - **Visual Studio** (Windows only): A professional IDE with great support for C++ game development.

    - **Code::Blocks**: A lightweight, cross-platform IDE that's perfect for beginners.

    - **CLion**: A paid, but powerful, cross-platform IDE that supports C++ development.

  - **Game Engine (Optional for Advanced Learning):**

    - **Unreal Engine:** If you plan to dive into game engines, Unreal Engine is the **industry standard** and **uses C++ extensively**.

    - **SFML (Simple and Fast Multimedia Library):** A great choice for building small games from scratch with C++.

- **Hardware**:

    o **PC with 8GB RAM or more**: This will ensure you can handle development without slowing down your system.

    o **Graphics Card** (Optional for 3D Game Development): A dedicated graphics card is important for building games that require high-end rendering.

Tip: If you're just starting, you don't need the most powerful computer. As you progress, your hardware requirements may increase, but for now, any modern laptop or desktop should suffice.

Installing Visual Studio

If you're using Visual Studio, here are the steps to set it up:

1. **Download Visual Studio** from the official website.

2. **Install the C++ Development Workload**:

    o During the installation, make sure to select the **Desktop development with C++** option.

    o This will install everything you need to develop games using C++.

Installing Code::Blocks

If you prefer a lighter, more straightforward IDE, follow these steps for **Code::Blocks**:

1. **Download Code::Blocks** from the official website.

2. **Install it,** making sure to include the **MinGW compiler** if you're using Windows (this is required to compile your C++ code).

Your First Project: Building a Simple "Hello, World!" Game

With your development environment ready, let's get coding! The best way to begin is by creating a simple program—a "Hello, World!" game.

Step 1: Create a New Project

1. Open your IDE (Visual Studio or Code::Blocks).

2. Create a new project. If you're using **Visual Studio**, choose a **Console Application**. If you're using **Code::Blocks**, choose **Console Application**, and make sure to select C++ as the language.

Step 2: Write the Code

In your main C++ file (typically **main.cpp**), type the following code:

#include <iostream> // This allows us to use standard input and output

```
int main() {
    // This line prints text to the screen
    std::cout << "Hello, World!" << std::endl;
    return 0;
}
```

Step 3: Compile and Run

- **Visual Studio**: Press Ctrl + F5 to build and run the program.

- **Code::Blocks**: Click the **Build and Run** button in the toolbar.

You should see the output: **"Hello, World!"**

What's Happening Here?

Let's break it down:

- #include <iostream>: This tells the program to include a library that handles input and output operations, like printing text to the screen.

- std::cout: This is the standard output stream in C++. It's what we use to print to the console.

- return 0;: This indicates the program finished successfully.

Congratulations! You just built your first **C++ program**! While this is just the beginning, it sets the stage for more complex games where you'll interact with players, respond to inputs, and create rich, immersive worlds.

Chapter 2: C++ Fundamentals for Game Development

Introduction

In Chapter 1, we took the first step in our game development journey by introducing C++ and setting up our development environment. Now, we're diving into the core concepts of **C++ fundamentals**. These are the building blocks you'll use in **every game you develop**, whether it's a small project or a complex AAA title. Understanding how **variables, data types**, and **functions** work is essential for crafting functional and interactive games.

We will break things down into manageable chunks, building up your knowledge step by step. Don't worry if some of the concepts seem unfamiliar—I'll guide you through everything with **hands-on projects, clear explanations**, and **engaging examples** to make the learning process fun and interactive.

By the end of this chapter, you'll have a solid understanding of how to:

- **Use variables and data types** in your games

- **Implement operators** for arithmetic, comparisons, and logical operations

- **Work with control structures** like **if-else** statements and **loops**

- **Create a simple game** that uses all these fundamental concepts!

What You'll Need: Software and Hardware Suggestions

Before we dive into the theory, make sure your development environment is ready:

- **Software**:

    - o **IDE (Integrated Development Environment)**: Use Visual Studio, Code::Blocks, or CLion. I recommend **Visual Studio** for its excellent debugging tools, especially for beginners.

    - o **Compiler**: Make sure your IDE has a C++ compiler set up. Visual Studio will automatically set this up for you.

- **Hardware**:

    - o A **modern computer** (laptop or desktop) with at least 4GB of RAM and a dual-core processor should suffice for game development. More powerful hardware is always better, but we'll start simple.

Variables, Data Types, and Functions

1. Variables

A **variable** is a container in memory where you can store data that can change over time during the program's execution. In game development, variables are essential to store things like a player's **score**, the **health** of a character, or the **position** of an object in your game.

In C++, each variable has a **type**, which determines the kind of data it can hold.

Declaring and Using Variables

To declare a variable in C++, you need to specify the **data type** and the **variable name**.

int score; // Declaring an integer variable named 'score'

score = 0; // Assigning a value to 'score'

double playerHealth = 100.0; // Declaring and initializing a double variable 'playerHealth'

In this example:

- **int** is a data type used for **integer values** (whole numbers).
- **double** is a data type used for **floating-point values** (decimals).

Common Data Types in C++

- **int**: Integer type (used for counting or whole numbers).
- **double**: Used for decimal values or floating-point numbers.
- **char**: Represents a single character (like 'A', '3', etc.).
- **bool**: Represents a boolean value (true or false).
- **string**: Used for text (a sequence of characters).

Example:

Let's say you are working on a simple RPG game where you need to track a player's **health, mana**, and **score**. You could declare these variables as follows:

int health = 100;

int mana = 50;

int score = 0;

2. Functions

In C++, a **function** is a block of code that performs a specific task. Functions help you organize your code and make it more reusable. Instead of repeating the same code multiple times, you define a function and call it whenever you need that specific task.

Creating Functions

Here's how you can create a basic function:

void greetPlayer() {

   std::cout << "Welcome to the game!" << std::endl;

}

In this example:

- **void** indicates that the function doesn't return any value.

- The function greetPlayer() prints a welcome message when called.

Calling Functions

Once a function is defined, you can **call** it in your program wherever you need it. For example, in your game's main loop, you might call greetPlayer() to display a greeting to the player at the start.

int main() {

   greetPlayer(); // Calling the function to greet the player

   return 0;

}

Functions with Parameters and Return Values

Some functions need **inputs** (called **parameters**) to perform a task, and they might return a **value**. Let's create a function to calculate the damage dealt by a player:

```
int calculateDamage(int baseDamage, int bonusDamage) {
    int totalDamage = baseDamage + bonusDamage;
    return totalDamage;
}
```

Here, calculateDamage() takes two integers (baseDamage and bonusDamage) as inputs, adds them together, and returns the result.

Operators: Arithmetic, Relational, and Logical Operators

Operators are essential tools that allow you to perform operations on variables and constants.

1. Arithmetic Operators

These operators allow you to perform basic mathematical operations.

- **+**: Addition

- **-**: Subtraction

- *****: Multiplication

- **/**: Division

- **%**: Modulo (remainder of division)

Example:

```
int a = 5;
```

```
int b = 2;
int sum = a + b;  // sum is 7
int product = a * b;  // product is 10
int remainder = a % b;  // remainder is 1
```

2. Relational Operators

Relational operators compare two values and return a boolean value (true or false).

- **==**: Equal to
- **!=**: Not equal to
- **>**: Greater than
- **<**: Less than
- **>=**: Greater than or equal to
- **<=**: Less than or equal to

Example:

```
int a = 5;
int b = 10;
bool result = a < b;  // result is true
```

3. Logical Operators

Logical operators are used to combine multiple conditions or negate a condition.

- **&&**: Logical AND

- **||**: Logical OR

- **!**: Logical NOT

Example:

```
bool playerAlive = true;
bool hasWeapon = false;
if (playerAlive && hasWeapon) {
    std::cout << "Player is ready to fight!" << std::endl;
} else {
    std::cout << "Player is unprepared!" << std::endl;
}
```

Control Structures: If-Else Statements and Loops

1. If-Else Statements

The **if-else** structure allows you to make decisions in your code. If a condition is true, the code inside the **if** block is executed. Otherwise, the code inside the **else** block is executed.

Example:

```
int playerHealth = 50;
```

```cpp
if (playerHealth > 0) {
    std::cout << "The player is alive!" << std::endl;
} else {
    std::cout << "The player is dead!" << std::endl;
}
```

2. Loops:

Loops allow you to repeat a block of code multiple times, which is especially useful in game development for tasks like updating game objects every frame.

For Loop

A **for loop** is typically used when you know how many times you need to repeat an action.

```cpp
for (int i = 0; i < 5; i++) {
    std::cout << "Iteration: " << i << std::endl;
}
```

While Loop

A **while loop** repeats an action as long as a condition remains true.

```cpp
int playerHealth = 100;
while (playerHealth > 0) {
    playerHealth -= 10;  // Decrease health by 10 each time
    std::cout << "Player Health: " << playerHealth << std::endl;
}
```

Hands-On Project: Building a Simple Number-Guessing Game

Now, let's put everything you've learned together with a hands-on project. You'll build a **number-guessing game** where the player tries to guess a number between 1 and 100. The game will give feedback based on whether the guess is too high, too low, or correct.

Step 1: Setup the Game

Start by defining the basic variables:

- The secret number (which the player will try to guess).

- The player's guess.

- The number of attempts.

```cpp
#include <iostream>
#include <cstdlib>  // For random number generation
#include <ctime>    // For seeding the random number generator


int main() {
    srand(time(0));  // Seed the random number generator
    int secretNumber = rand() % 100 + 1;  // Generate a secret number between 1 and 100
    int playerGuess = 0;
    int attempts = 0;


    std::cout << "Welcome to the Number Guessing Game!" << std::endl;
    std::cout << "Try to guess the number between 1 and 100." << std::endl;
```

```cpp
while (playerGuess != secretNumber) {
    std::cout << "Enter your guess: ";
    std::cin >> playerGuess;
    attempts++;

    if (playerGuess < secretNumber) {
        std::cout << "Too low! Try again." << std::endl;
    } else if (playerGuess > secretNumber) {
        std::cout << "Too high! Try again." << std::endl;
    } else {
        std::cout << "Congratulations! You guessed the correct number in " << attempts << " attempts!" << std::endl;
    }
}

return 0;
}
```

Step 2: Explanation of the Code

- **Variables**: secretNumber, playerGuess, and attempts store the number to guess, the player's guess, and the number of attempts, respectively.

- **Control Structures**: The while loop repeats until the player guesses the correct number, and the if-else statements give feedback based on the guess.

- **Functions**: We use the rand() function to generate a random secret number between 1 and 100.

Step 3: Run and Test the Game

Now, compile and run the game. The player should input guesses, and the game should provide feedback until they guess the correct number.

Conclusion

In this chapter, we covered the essential building blocks of C++ programming for game development, including **variables, data types, functions, operators**, and **control structures**. We put all of these concepts into practice by creating a simple **number-guessing game**.

You now have the knowledge to start building interactive and dynamic games! In the next chapter, we will explore more advanced concepts, including **object-oriented programming** (OOP), which is crucial for structuring your game efficiently.

Chapter 3: Object-Oriented Programming (OOP) in C++

Introduction to Object-Oriented Programming (OOP)

In the world of game development, **object-oriented programming (OOP)** is the backbone of how games are structured. As a game developer, understanding how to apply the principles of OOP is essential for building scalable, maintainable, and organized code. In this chapter, we're going to dive deep into the fundamentals of OOP, specifically in **C++**, and explore how it can help you organize and manage complex systems within your game.

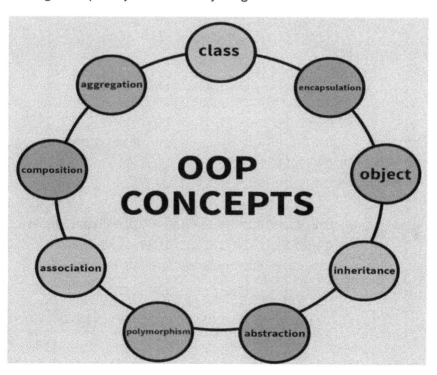

Whether you're building a **small indie game** or a **massive AAA game**, OOP principles like **classes, objects, encapsulation, inheritance**, and **polymorphism** will allow you to design clean and modular code. These concepts will help you manage everything from player characters to game mechanics and artificial intelligence.

By the end of this chapter, you'll be able to:

1. **Define and use classes and objects** in C++.

2. Understand key OOP principles: **Encapsulation, Inheritance**, and **Polymorphism**.

3. **Distinguish between static and dynamic memory allocation** and know when to use each.

4. Create a **Monster class** for your game with various properties like health, damage, and movement.

Let's dive right in!

What You'll Need

Before we dive into the details, let's quickly ensure you have everything you need for this chapter:

- **Software:**

    - **IDE:** You should be using an **IDE** like **Visual Studio, Code::Blocks**, or **CLion**. For this chapter, we'll assume you're familiar with setting up your IDE.

    - **C++ Compiler:** Make sure your C++ compiler is correctly set up with your IDE (most IDEs handle this automatically).

- **Hardware:**

- A **laptop or desktop** with at least **4GB of RAM** should be sufficient. As you advance, larger games will require more resources, but for now, this is enough.

---

1. Classes and Objects: The Core of OOP

In object-oriented programming, the **class** is the blueprint for creating objects. An object is an **instance** of a class. Think of a class as a **template** and an object as an **actual instance** that can perform tasks or hold data.

What is a Class?

A **class** defines the properties (called **attributes**) and behaviors (called **methods**) that an object created from that class will have. For example, imagine you're creating a **Monster** for your game. The Monster class could define properties such as **health**, **damage**, and **name**, and methods like **attack()** and **move()**.

Here's a simple example of a **Monster class**:

```cpp
#include <iostream>
#include <string>

class Monster {
public:
    // Properties (attributes)
    std::string name;
    int health;
    int damage;
```

```
    // Method (behavior)
    void attack() {
        std::cout << name << "attacks and deals " << damage << "
damage!" << std::endl;
    }

    void move() {
        std::cout << name << "moves forward!" << std::endl;
    }
};
```

In this example:

- **name, health,** and **damage** are the **attributes.**
- **attack()** and **move()** are the **methods.**

Creating Objects

Once you have a class defined, you can create **objects** that are instances of that class. Here's how to create a **Monster** object:

```
int main() {
    // Creating an object of class Monster
    Monster goblin;

    // Setting the attributes of the goblin object
    goblin.name = "Goblin";
    goblin.health = 100;
    goblin.damage = 15;
```

```
// Calling methods on the goblin object
goblin.attack();
goblin.move();

return 0;
}
```

In this code:

- We create an object **goblin** of the **Monster** class.

- We assign values to its **name, health**, and **damage** properties.

- We call the **attack()** and **move()** methods to simulate the goblin's behavior.

Understanding the Relationship Between Classes and Objects

- **Classes** are **blueprints** that define the structure and behavior of objects.

- **Objects** are **instances** of these blueprints that hold specific data and can perform actions.

---

2. Encapsulation: Protecting Data

Encapsulation is one of the key principles of object-oriented programming. It's the concept of **bundling** the data (attributes) and the methods (functions) that work on that data into a **single unit** or class. It also involves restricting direct access to some of the object's components, which is done using **access modifiers**.

Access Modifiers: Public, Private, and Protected

- **public**: Members that are accessible from outside the class.

- **private**: Members that are not accessible from outside the class.

- **protected**: Similar to private, but can be accessed by subclasses.

Example of Encapsulation:

```
class Monster {
private:
    int health; // Private variable, can't be accessed directly outside the class


public:
    // Getter method to access health
    int getHealth() {
        return health;
    }


    // Setter method to set health
    void setHealth(int h) {
        if (h > 0) { // Ensuring health cannot be set to a negative value
            health = h;
        }
```

```
    }

    void attack() {

        std::cout << "Monster attacks!" << std::endl;

    }
};
```

In this example:

- The **health** variable is private, meaning it cannot be accessed directly from outside the class.

- We provide **getter** and **setter** methods to control how health is accessed and modified. This is a common OOP practice known as **data hiding**.

---

3. Inheritance: Reusing Code

Inheritance allows one class to **inherit** properties and behaviors from another class. This promotes **code reuse** and helps you organize your game code more efficiently.

What is Inheritance?

Inheritance enables a new class (called a **derived class**) to take on the attributes and methods of an existing class (called a **base class**). You can add new properties and methods, or modify existing ones.

For example, let's create a **Zombie** class that inherits from the **Monster** class.

Example of Inheritance:

```
class Monster {
```

```cpp
public:
    std::string name;
    int health;
    int damage;

    void attack() {
        std::cout << name << " attacks and deals " << damage << " damage!" << std::endl;
    }
};


class Zombie : public Monster {
public:
    void groan() {
        std::cout << name << " groans ominously!" << std::endl;
    }
};
```

Here:

- **Zombie** is a derived class that inherits from **Monster**.

- **Zombie** can **attack()** like a **Monster**, but it also has its own unique behavior: **groan()**.

Using Inheritance:

```cpp
int main() {
    Zombie zombie;
    zombie.name = "Zombie";
```

```
zombie.health = 50;
zombie.damage = 10;

zombie.attack();  // Inherited method
zombie.groan();   // Zombie-specific method

return 0;
}
```

- The **Zombie** object can attack (inherited from **Monster**) and groan (unique to **Zombie**).

The Power of Inheritance

Inheritance lets you create specialized versions of existing classes without rewriting code. In game development, you might have a base **Character** class, and then have **Player** and **NPC** (Non-Player Character) subclasses that share common behavior but also have their own specific features.

---

4. Polymorphism: One Interface, Multiple Implementations

Polymorphism allows objects of different classes to be treated as objects of a common base class. The most common use of polymorphism is when a **base class reference or pointer** is used to call methods of a derived class.

What is Polymorphism?

Polymorphism is the ability of different classes to implement methods with the same name but with different behaviors. In simpler terms, you can have the same method name in different classes, but each class can perform the method in its own way.

Example of Polymorphism:

```cpp
class Monster {
public:
    virtual void attack() {
        std::cout << "Monster attacks!" << std::endl;
    }
};


class Zombie : public Monster {
public:
    void attack() override {
        std::cout << "Zombie attacks with a bite!" << std::endl;
    }
};


class Goblin : public Monster {
public:
    void attack() override {
        std::cout << "Goblin attacks with a club!" << std::endl;
    }
};
```

In this code:

- We use **virtual** in the base class method **attack()**. This tells C++ that the method might be overridden in derived classes.

- **override** in derived classes (like **Zombie** and **Goblin**) ensures we are properly overriding the base class's method.

Using Polymorphism:

```
int main() {
    Monster* monsterPtr;
    Zombie zombie;
    Goblin goblin;

    monsterPtr = &zombie;
    monsterPtr->attack();  // Calls Zombie's attack

    monsterPtr = &goblin;
    monsterPtr->attack();  // Calls Goblin's attack

    return 0;
}
```

- The **attack()** method behaves differently depending on whether it's called on a **Zombie** or a **Goblin**.

Why Polymorphism is Powerful

Polymorphism allows you to **extend your game** easily. For example, you can add new types of monsters (like **Vampires** or **Witches**) without needing to modify your existing game logic. All monsters can be treated the same way, but each can have its own unique **attack()** behavior.

5. Static vs Dynamic Memory Allocation

Understanding memory allocation is key to managing resources efficiently in game development.

Static Memory Allocation

In static memory allocation, the memory is allocated at compile-time. These variables exist throughout the program's lifetime.

- **Example**: Local variables inside a function or **global variables**.

int score = 0; // Static memory allocation

Dynamic Memory Allocation

Dynamic memory allocation happens at runtime using **new** or **malloc**. This is more flexible and is used for creating objects whose size or number cannot be determined at compile-time.

- **Example**: Creating a **Monster** object dynamically.

Monster* monster = new Monster; // Dynamically allocate memory for a Monster

monster->name = "Dragon";

monster->health = 200;

When to Use Each Type

- **Static allocation** is ideal for fixed, known values (like a player's score or the number of lives).

- **Dynamic allocation** is useful when the size or number of objects cannot be predetermined (like dynamically spawning monsters during the game).

Hands-On Project: Create a Simple "Monster" Class

Now, let's put everything we've learned into action by creating a simple **Monster** class for your game. This class will include properties like **health**, **damage**, and **movement**, as well as methods to interact with these properties.

Step 1: Define the Monster Class

```
#include <iostream>
#include <string>

class Monster {
private:
    int health;
    int damage;

public:
    std::string name;

    Monster(std::string n, int h, int d) {
        name = n;
        health = h;
        damage = d;
    }
```

```cpp
    void attack() {
        std::cout << name << "attacks and deals " << damage << "
damage!" << std::endl;
    }


    void takeDamage(int damageTaken) {
        health -= damageTaken;
        if (health < 0) health = 0;
        std::cout << name << "now has " << health << "health!" <<
std::endl;
    }


    void move() {
        std::cout << name << "moves forward!" << std::endl;
    }


    int getHealth() {
        return health;
    }
};
```

Step 2: Use the Monster Class

```cpp
int main() {
    Monster goblin("Goblin", 100, 20);
    goblin.attack();
    goblin.move();
    goblin.takeDamage(30);
```

```
std::cout << "Goblin's current health: " << goblin.getHealth() <<
std::endl;

    return 0;
}
```

Step 3: Explanation

- We define the **Monster** class with **health**, **damage**, and **name** as properties.

- **Methods**: The **attack()**, **takeDamage()**, and **move()** methods allow the monster to perform actions.

- We create a **Goblin** object with specific values for health and damage and simulate its actions.

Conclusion

In this chapter, you've learned the fundamentals of **object-oriented programming (OOP)** in C++, including the key concepts of **classes**, **objects**, **encapsulation**, **inheritance**, **polymorphism**, and **memory allocation**. We applied these concepts to build a **Monster class** for your game, laying the groundwork for more complex game systems.

The power of OOP lies in its ability to help you build **modular**, **scalable**, and **maintainable** game code. With a solid understanding of these principles, you're now ready to take on more advanced game development concepts and continue building your game.

Chapter 4: Working with C++ Libraries and Tools

Introduction

In game development, efficient coding is key to delivering performance, fluidity, and scalability. As your game grows in complexity, managing data and rendering graphics becomes more challenging. That's where **C++ libraries and tools** come in. In this chapter, we will dive into two fundamental aspects of C++ development for games: the **Standard Template Library (STL)** and **third-party libraries** like **SDL, OpenGL,** and **SFML**.

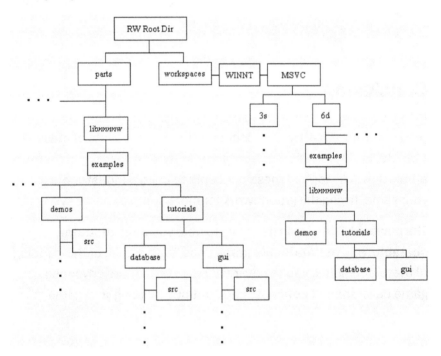

By understanding how to effectively use these tools, you'll be able to:

1. Handle and store complex game data using **STL containers** like **vectors**, **maps**, and **iterators**.

2. Create game graphics and build interactive windows with libraries like **SDL** or **SFML**.

3. Implement basic game windows to lay the foundation for more advanced graphics programming.

By the end of this chapter, you'll have a practical, hands-on project— a **game window** using **SDL2** or **SFML**—to test your understanding and kick-start your game development journey.

What You'll Need

Before diving into the content, let's make sure you have the necessary tools to follow along:

Software

- **IDE (Integrated Development Environment)**: You can use **Visual Studio**, **Code::Blocks**, or **CLion** for this chapter.

- **C++ Compiler**: Ensure your IDE is set up with the C++ compiler. Visual Studio has this setup by default.

- **SDL2 or SFML**: These are the libraries we will be using for creating graphical windows.

  - **SDL2**: A low-level graphics library that is perfect for game development.

  - **SFML**: A slightly higher-level library that simplifies many aspects of SDL, like audio and networking.

Hardware

- A **laptop or desktop** with at least **4GB of RAM** and a **dual-core processor** will work perfectly. However, for more intensive game projects, stronger hardware would be beneficial.

- **Graphics Card (Optional)**: For advanced rendering, a dedicated GPU may become important, but for the purposes of this chapter, integrated graphics should suffice.

The Standard Template Library (STL)

C++'s **Standard Template Library (STL)** is an invaluable tool for game developers. It provides efficient, pre-built **data structures** and **algorithms** that help manage and manipulate data. Let's start by understanding the key **STL containers** that you'll frequently use in game development.

1. Vectors: Dynamic Arrays

A **vector** is a dynamic array that can grow or shrink in size. It's used to store data that might change in size during runtime—such as storing all the monsters in your game or collecting user input over time.

Using Vectors:

```cpp
#include <iostream>
#include <vector>

int main() {
    std::vector<int> scores; // Declare a vector to store integers
```

```
// Adding elements to the vector
scores.push_back(10);  // Add score 10
scores.push_back(20);  // Add score 20
scores.push_back(30);  // Add score 30

// Accessing elements
for (int i = 0; i < scores.size(); i++) {
    std::cout << "Score " << i+1 << ": " << scores[i] << std::endl;
}

return 0;
}
```

What's Happening?

- **push_back()** adds elements to the end of the vector.

- The **size()** function returns the number of elements in the vector.

- **scores[i]** accesses each element by index.

Vectors are great for situations where you need a flexible container to hold an unpredictable number of items.

2. Maps: Key-Value Pairs

A **map** is a container that stores data in **key-value pairs**. It's perfect for storing data where you need to quickly look up a value based on a unique key—like a player's score or inventory items.

Using Maps:

```cpp
#include <iostream>
#include <map>

int main() {
    std::map<std::string, int> playerScores;

    // Adding key-value pairs to the map
    playerScores["Alice"] = 50;
    playerScores["Bob"] = 70;
    playerScores["Charlie"] = 30;

    // Accessing values by keys
    for (auto& player : playerScores) {
        std::cout << player.first << " has a score of " << player.second << std::endl;
    }

    return 0;
}
```

What's Happening?

- The map stores **string** keys and **integer** values, representing players' names and their scores.

- You can iterate through the map using a **range-based for loop** to print out all player scores.

Maps are essential when you need to quickly access data based on a specific identifier, like **player IDs**, **item names**, or **level names**.

3. Iterators: Navigating Through Containers

An **iterator** is an object that points to an element in a container. It's like a pointer but is used in STL containers to help you navigate through and manipulate elements in containers like **vectors**, **maps**, and **lists**.

Using Iterators:

```cpp
#include <iostream>
#include <vector>

int main() {
    std::vector<int> scores = {10, 20, 30};

    // Creating an iterator
    std::vector<int>::iterator it;

    // Iterating through the vector using the iterator
    for (it = scores.begin(); it != scores.end(); ++it) {
        std::cout << "Score: " << *it << std::endl;
    }

    return 0;
}
```

What's Happening?

- **scores.begin()** returns an iterator that points to the first element in the vector.

- **scores.end()** returns an iterator that points just past the last element.

- The *it dereferences the iterator to access the value it points to.

Iterators are critical for traversing and manipulating data within any container type in STL.

Third-Party Libraries for Game Development

While STL containers help you handle data efficiently, third-party libraries like **SDL2**, **SFML**, and **OpenGL** are designed to handle complex tasks like **graphics rendering**, **audio management**, and **event handling**—key components of any game engine.

1. SDL2 (Simple DirectMedia Layer 2)

SDL2 is a powerful, cross-platform library designed for game development. It provides tools for handling **graphics**, **audio**, **keyboard/mouse input**, and **window management**. If you're looking for a low-level library with a strong focus on 2D game development, SDL2 is a great choice.

Setting Up SDL2:

Before we start writing code, you'll need to install SDL2 on your system:

- Download the appropriate version of SDL2 from the official SDL website and set it up in your IDE.

- Link SDL2 to your project (follow the SDL2 documentation for detailed installation instructions).

2. SFML (Simple and Fast Multimedia Library)

SFML is a higher-level graphics library that builds on SDL2 but offers easier-to-use abstractions for managing window creation, sprites, textures, and more. It's ideal for **2D games** and is a great starting point for newcomers.

Setting Up SFML:

- Download SFML from the official website and set it up in your IDE.

- Include the necessary **SFML headers** and link to the required libraries.

3. OpenGL: Low-Level Graphics Rendering

OpenGL is a powerful low-level graphics API used for rendering 2D and 3D graphics. It's widely used for **AAA games** and **game engines** due to its performance and flexibility.

While OpenGL can be more complex to use than SDL2 or SFML, it provides fine-grained control over how graphics are rendered, which is crucial for building high-performance, 3D games.

Hands-On Project: Implement a Basic Game Window Using SDL2 or SFML

In this hands-on project, we'll use **SDL2** (although SFML would follow a very similar approach) to create a basic game window and display a simple color on the screen.

Step 1: Initializing SDL2

The first step is to initialize SDL and create a window:

#include <SDL2/SDL.h>

```cpp
#include <iostream>

int main() {
    if (SDL_Init(SDL_INIT_VIDEO) < 0) {
        std::cout << "SDL could not initialize! SDL_Error: " <<
SDL_GetError() << std::endl;
        return -1;
    }


    // Create window
    SDL_Window* window = SDL_CreateWindow("Basic Game
Window", SDL_WINDOWPOS_UNDEFINED,
SDL_WINDOWPOS_UNDEFINED, 800, 600,
SDL_WINDOW_SHOWN);
    if (!window) {
        std::cout << "Window could not be created! SDL_Error: " <<
SDL_GetError() << std::endl;
        return -1;
    }


    // Get window surface
    SDL_Surface* screenSurface =
SDL_GetWindowSurface(window);


    // Fill the surface with a color
    SDL_FillRect(screenSurface, NULL,
SDL_MapRGB(screenSurface->format, 0x00, 0x00, 0xFF)); // Blue
background
```

```
// Update the window
SDL_UpdateWindowSurface(window);

// Wait for 2 seconds
SDL_Delay(2000);

// Clean up and close SDL
SDL_DestroyWindow(window);
SDL_Quit();

return 0;
}
```

Step 2: Explanation of the Code

- **SDL_Init(SDL_INIT_VIDEO)** initializes the SDL video subsystem.

- **SDL_CreateWindow** creates a window with the title "Basic Game Window" of size **800x600**.

- **SDL_GetWindowSurface** gets the window's surface, which is the area where graphics can be drawn.

- **SDL_FillRect** fills the window with a color (in this case, **blue**).

- **SDL_UpdateWindowSurface** updates the window to display the filled color.

- **SDL_Delay** keeps the window open for **2 seconds** before closing.

Step 3: Running the Code

Once the code is compiled and executed, you should see a **blue window** for 2 seconds before it closes. This is the foundation for many games, as it gives you a window where you can start drawing objects, handling events, and building game logic.

Conclusion

In this chapter, we covered:

- How to use **STL containers** like **vectors** and **maps** to efficiently store and manage game data.

- An introduction to third-party libraries such as **SDL2**, **SFML**, and **OpenGL**, which are critical for handling **graphics**, **input**, and **window management** in games.

- A hands-on project where you built a **basic game window** using SDL2, setting the stage for creating interactive, graphical games.

By leveraging the power of these libraries and tools, you can handle more complex game systems and focus on the fun part: creating engaging gameplay experiences.

Now that you have a solid understanding of **C++ libraries** and **game tools**, you're ready to continue building your game with more advanced concepts and features in the upcoming chapters.

Chapter 5: Advanced C++ Features

Introduction to Advanced C++ Features

As we continue building more complex games, we must look deeper into C++ and its advanced features that allow us to write **more efficient, cleaner,** and **more maintainable** code. In this chapter, we'll focus on some powerful C++ features that are crucial for handling **complex game systems**, particularly those that involve **memory management, performance optimization,** and **code simplification**. These features are:

- **Smart Pointers**: To manage memory effectively and avoid **memory leaks**.

- **Lambda Functions**: To simplify code and make it more readable.

- **Move Semantics**: To enhance performance, especially in memory-intensive applications like games.

By the end of this chapter, you'll have learned how to use these features to refactor memory-intensive parts of your game, improve performance, and avoid common pitfalls.

What You'll Need

Before diving into the code examples, make sure you have everything set up:

Software:

- **IDE (Integrated Development Environment)**: Visual Studio, CLion, or Code::Blocks are ideal for C++ development. Ensure your IDE has the latest C++ compiler and supports modern C++ standards (C++11 and later).

- **C++ Compiler**: You'll need a C++11 or later compliant compiler for this chapter. Most modern IDEs handle this automatically.

- **Operating System**: This chapter works on all major operating systems—Windows, Linux, and macOS. Ensure your system has a C++ development environment set up.

Hardware:

- A **laptop or desktop** with **4GB of RAM** is sufficient for this chapter. However, if you're planning to work on more demanding game projects later, more RAM and a **dedicated graphics card** may be helpful.

---

1. Smart Pointers: Managing Memory Safely

Memory management is one of the most critical aspects of game development. In C++, the traditional way of managing memory is through **pointers**, but using raw pointers can often lead to **memory leaks**, where allocated memory is not freed, causing your game to use up more and more memory as it runs.

Luckily, C++11 introduced **smart pointers**, which automatically manage memory, ensuring that memory is properly released when it's no longer needed. This reduces the chances of memory leaks and makes memory management much safer and easier.

What Are Smart Pointers?

Smart pointers are wrappers around regular pointers, and they automatically manage the memory of dynamically allocated objects. There are three types of smart pointers in C++:

1. **std::unique_ptr**: Represents **exclusive ownership** of an object. It can only have one owner, and when the unique pointer goes out of scope, the memory is automatically released.

2. **std::shared_ptr**: Represents **shared ownership** of an object. Multiple shared_ptr instances can point to the same object, and the memory is freed when the last shared_ptr is destroyed.

3. **std::weak_ptr**: Used in conjunction with shared_ptr, but it doesn't increase the reference count. It's useful for breaking **cyclic dependencies** in shared ownership scenarios.

Using std::unique_ptr

std::unique_ptr is used when you want a single owner for an object, and when the object goes out of scope, the memory is automatically freed.

Example of std::unique_ptr:

```cpp
#include <iostream>
#include <memory>


class Monster {
public:
    Monster() {
        std::cout << "Monster created!" << std::endl;
```

```
  }
  ~Monster() {
    std::cout << "Monster destroyed!" << std::endl;
  }
  void attack() {
    std::cout << "Monster attacks!" << std::endl;
  }
};

int main() {
  std::unique_ptr<Monster> goblin =
std::make_unique<Monster>(); // Unique ownership
  goblin->attack(); // Calling method on the unique pointer
  return 0; // goblin goes out of scope, and memory is freed
automatically
}
```

Explanation:

- std::make_unique<Monster>() creates a **unique pointer** to a Monster object.

- The memory is automatically freed when the unique_ptr goes out of scope at the end of the function.

Using std::shared_ptr

std::shared_ptr allows multiple pointers to share ownership of a dynamically allocated object. The object is destroyed when the last shared_ptr pointing to it is destroyed.

Example of std::shared_ptr:

```cpp
#include <iostream>
#include <memory>

class Monster {
public:
    Monster() {
        std::cout << "Monster created!" << std::endl;
    }
    ~Monster() {
        std::cout << "Monster destroyed!" << std::endl;
    }
    void attack() {
        std::cout << "Monster attacks!" << std::endl;
    }
};

int main() {
    std::shared_ptr<Monster> goblin1 = std::make_shared<Monster>();
    std::shared_ptr<Monster> goblin2 = goblin1; // Shared ownership

    goblin1->attack();
    goblin2->attack();
```

```
    std::cout << "Number of shared_ptr pointing to goblin: " <<
goblin1.use_count() << std::endl;


    return 0;  // Memory will be freed when the last shared_ptr is
destroyed

}
```

Explanation:

- goblin1 and goblin2 share ownership of the same Monster object.

- use_count() shows how many shared_ptr objects are pointing to the same resource.

- The object is destroyed when the last shared_ptr goes out of scope.

The Power of Smart Pointers in Game Development

Smart pointers help you manage memory automatically in game development, especially when dealing with complex game systems like **AI agents**, **game objects**, and **particles**. They ensure that the memory is properly freed when objects are no longer in use, reducing memory leaks and **segmentation faults**.

---

2. Lambda Functions: Simplifying Your Code

Lambda functions, introduced in C++11, allow you to define anonymous functions inline, without the need for a separate function declaration. They can be especially useful when you need small, short-lived functions that don't justify a full-fledged function definition.

What Are Lambda Functions?

A **lambda function** is a function that can be defined directly in the body of another function. It allows you to write code **in place** without needing to jump to a separate function definition.

Syntax of a Lambda Function:

[capture clause] (parameters) -> return type { function body }

- **Capture Clause**: Determines which variables are available inside the lambda.

- **Parameters**: The lambda's parameter list, similar to a regular function.

- **Return Type**: Optional, inferred by the compiler, but can be explicitly defined.

- **Function Body**: The code that gets executed when the lambda is called.

Example of a Lambda Function:

```cpp
#include <iostream>
#include <vector>

int main() {
    std::vector<int> numbers = {1, 2, 3, 4, 5};

    // Using a lambda function to sum all numbers in the vector
    int sum = 0;
    for (auto& num : numbers) {
        sum += num;
```

```
    }

    std::cout << "Sum: " << sum << std::endl;

    // Using a lambda for more specific operations (e.g., doubling
    numbers)
    auto doubleNumbers = [](int n) { return n * 2; };
    for (auto& num : numbers) {
        num = doubleNumbers(num);  // Doubling each number
    }

    std::cout << "Doubled Numbers: ";
    for (auto& num : numbers) {
        std::cout << num << " ";
    }
    std::cout << std::endl;

    return 0;
}
```

Explanation:

- The **lambda function** auto doubleNumbers = [](int n) { return n * 2; }; takes an integer and doubles it.

- The lambda is invoked within the loop to modify each element in the vector.

Why Use Lambda Functions in Game Development?

Lambda functions allow you to:

- **Write concise and inline functions** where they're needed.

- Use them with **STL algorithms** like std::sort(), std::for_each(), etc.

- Avoid unnecessary function declarations for small, one-time use cases.

---

3. Move Semantics: Optimizing Performance

When you deal with objects in C++, **move semantics** allow you to transfer ownership of resources from one object to another, rather than copying them. This is crucial for improving the performance of your game when dealing with large objects or resources like **game assets**.

What is Move Semantics?

C++11 introduced **move constructors** and **move assignment operators**, which allow for **efficient transfers** of resources. Instead of copying objects, you "move" the resources from one object to another.

- **Move Constructor**: Transfers ownership of resources from a source object to a new object.

- **Move Assignment Operator**: Transfers ownership when an object is assigned a new value.

Why Move Semantics Matter in Games

Games often have large objects—like textures, models, and audio files. Moving these objects instead of copying them reduces memory overhead and increases performance, especially in resource-heavy applications like games.

Move Constructor Example:

```
#include <iostream>
#include <vector>

class GameObject {
public:
    int* data;
    GameObject(int size) {
        data = new int[size]; // Dynamically allocate memory
        std::cout << "GameObject created!" << std::endl;
    }

    // Move constructor
    GameObject(GameObject&& other) noexcept {
        data = other.data; // Transfer ownership of data
        other.data = nullptr; // Leave the other object in a valid state
        std::cout << "GameObject moved!" << std::endl;
    }

    ~GameObject() {
        if (data) {
            delete[] data; // Clean up memory
            std::cout << "GameObject destroyed!" << std::endl;
```

```
        }
    }
};


int main() {
    GameObject obj1(100); // Create a GameObject
    GameObject obj2 = std::move(obj1); // Move obj1 to obj2

    // obj1 is in a valid but empty state now (data is nullptr)

    return 0;
}
```

Explanation:

- The move constructor **transfers** the ownership of data from obj1 to obj2, instead of copying it.

- After the move, obj1 is left in a valid state but with a null pointer for data.

Move Assignment Example:

```
GameObject obj1(100);
GameObject obj2(200);


// Move assignment
obj2 = std::move(obj1); // Transfers ownership of data from obj1 to obj2
```

Hands-On Project: Refactor a Game's Memory-Intensive Functions

Now, let's put everything we've learned into a practical project. Imagine you're working on a game where you need to manage multiple **GameObject** instances. We will **refactor a memory-intensive function** using **smart pointers** and **move semantics** to improve the game's performance.

Step 1: Initial Setup with Raw Pointers

```
#include <iostream>
#include <vector>

class GameObject {
public:
    int* data;

    GameObject(int size) {
        data = new int[size];
    }

    ~GameObject() {
        delete[] data;
    }
};

void createObjects(int numObjects) {
    std::vector<GameObject *> objects;
```

```
for (int i = 0; i < numObjects; i++) {
    objects.push_back(new GameObject(1000));
}

// Clean up memory
for (auto obj : objects) {
    delete obj;
    }
}

int main() {
    createObjects(1000);
    return 0;
}
```

In this example, memory is allocated dynamically for each GameObject using **raw pointers**. We manually clean up the memory by calling delete after using the objects.

Step 2: Refactor with Smart Pointers

Let's refactor the code to use **std::unique_ptr** to automatically manage memory.

```
#include <iostream>
#include <vector>
#include <memory>

class GameObject {
```

```cpp
public:
    int * data;

    GameObject(int size) {
        data = new int[size];
    }

    ~GameObject() {
        delete[] data;
    }
};

void createObjects(int numObjects) {
    std::vector<std::unique_ptr<GameObject>> objects;

    for (int i = 0; i < numObjects; i++) {
        objects.push_back(std::make_unique<GameObject>(1000));
    }

    // No need to manually delete the objects; memory is
    automatically cleaned up when they go out of scope.
}

int main() {
    createObjects(1000);
    return 0;
```

```
}
```

Step 3: Implement Move Semantics

Now, let's refactor the code to take advantage of **move semantics** to transfer ownership efficiently:

```cpp
#include <iostream>
#include <vector>
#include <memory>

class GameObject {
public:
    int* data;

    GameObject(int size) {
        data = new int[size];
    }

    // Move constructor
    GameObject(GameObject&& other) noexcept {
        data = other.data;
        other.data = nullptr;
    }

    ~GameObject() {
        delete[] data;
    }
```

```
};

void createObjects(int numObjects) {
    std::vector<GameObject> objects;

    for (int i = 0; i < numObjects; i++) {
        objects.push_back(GameObject(1000));  // Move the object
efficiently
    }
}

int main() {
    createObjects(1000);
    return 0;
}
```

Conclusion

In this chapter, we explored three **advanced C++ features**:

1. **Smart pointers**: Used to automatically manage memory and prevent memory leaks.

2. **Lambda functions**: Simplified the code, making it more concise and readable.

3. **Move semantics**: Allowed us to efficiently transfer resources between objects, improving performance.

You've now learned how to manage complex game systems efficiently by applying these advanced features. By implementing **smart pointers** and **move semantics**, you can handle memory-intensive objects without the risk of leaks or unnecessary copies, ultimately making your game more performant and maintainable.

Chapter 6: Memory Management and Optimization

Introduction

In game development, **memory management** is one of the most critical aspects of building high-performance, reliable applications. As games become larger and more complex, efficient memory management ensures that the game runs smoothly without consuming unnecessary resources. Improper memory handling can lead to **memory leaks**, causing your game to slow down or even crash, especially as the game progresses and more data is loaded.

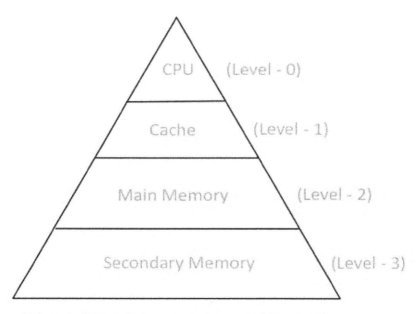

Hierarchical representation of Memory

In this chapter, we will focus on **manual memory management** using **pointers** and **dynamic memory** in C++, explore how to **avoid memory leaks**, and delve into **profiling tools** to monitor your game's performance. We'll wrap up with a **hands-on project** where we will optimize a game loop, apply **memory pools**, and fix **memory leaks**.

By the end of this chapter, you will be equipped with the skills needed to manage memory efficiently and make your game more optimized and scalable.

What You'll Need

Before we dive into the concepts, ensure your development environment is ready:

Software

- **IDE (Integrated Development Environment)**: You should be using a C++ IDE like **Visual Studio, CLion**, or **Code::Blocks** for ease of use.

- **C++ Compiler**: Ensure your compiler supports C++11 or later (Visual Studio, for example, handles this automatically).

- **Profiling Tools**: Install profiling tools like **Valgrind** (Linux), **Visual Studio Profiler** (Windows), or **gprof** (Linux and macOS) for performance tracking and memory analysis.

Hardware

- **4GB RAM or more**: While 4GB of RAM should suffice for most C++ game development, having more memory will help when working on larger games.

- **Modern CPU**: For game development and performance profiling, a dual-core or higher processor is recommended.

---

1. Manual Memory Management in C++

Memory management is one of C++'s most powerful but tricky features. While languages like Python or Java handle memory management automatically, C++ gives you **direct control** over memory allocation and deallocation. Understanding **pointers** and **dynamic memory allocation** is essential for creating efficient games.

Pointers: The Basics

A **pointer** in C++ is a variable that stores the memory address of another variable. Instead of working with actual data, a pointer points to the location in memory where the data is stored.

Declaring Pointers:

int * ptr; // Pointer to an integer

int var = 5;

ptr = &var; // Pointer 'ptr' now stores the address of 'var'

In the above example:

- **ptr** is a pointer that can hold the address of an integer.

- The **&** operator is used to get the **address** of a variable.

Dynamic Memory Allocation

When working with larger data structures, we often don't know how much memory is needed at compile time. This is where **dynamic memory allocation** comes in. You can allocate memory during runtime using new and delete.

Using new and delete:

```cpp
#include <iostream>

int main() {
    int* ptr = new int; // Allocate memory for one integer
    *ptr = 10; // Assign value to the allocated memory
    std::cout << *ptr << std::endl; // Output: 10

    delete ptr; // Deallocate memory
    return 0;
}
```

Explanation:

- **new** allocates memory on the heap.

- **delete** deallocates that memory when you're done using it.

- Not calling delete results in a **memory leak**, as the memory is never freed.

Arrays and Dynamic Memory

For more complex data structures like arrays, we can also use **dynamic arrays**. You can allocate a block of memory large enough to hold multiple elements, and then deallocate it when it's no longer needed.

```cpp
#include <iostream>

int main() {
```

```
int * arr = new int[5]; // Allocate memory for an array of 5
integers

for (int i = 0; i < 5; i++) {
    arr[i] = i * 2; // Assign values to the array
}

for (int i = 0; i < 5; i++) {
    std::cout << arr[i] << " "; // Output: 0 2 4 6 8
}
std::cout << std::endl;

delete[] arr; // Deallocate memory for the array
return 0;
}
```

Explanation:

- The **new[]** operator allocates memory for an array.

- The **delete[]** operator deallocates memory for an array.

---

2. Avoiding Memory Leaks

Memory leaks occur when memory is allocated dynamically but never freed, causing the system to run out of memory over time. Proper memory management is critical for long-running applications like games.

Best Practices to Avoid Memory Leaks

1. **Always delete memory after use**: When you allocate memory with new, ensure that you call delete (or delete[] for arrays) to free the memory.

2. **Use smart pointers**: Modern C++ encourages the use of **smart pointers** (std::unique_ptr and std::shared_ptr), which automatically manage memory and ensure it's freed when it's no longer in use. Using smart pointers reduces the risk of memory leaks and eliminates the need for manual memory management in most cases.

3. **Track memory usage**: Keep track of memory allocations to prevent accidental multiple allocations without freeing memory. This is especially important for **game objects** that are created and destroyed frequently.

Memory Leaks Example:

```cpp
#include <iostream>


class Monster {
public:
    int* health;
    Monster() {
        health = new int(100);  // Dynamically allocated memory
    }
```

```
~Monster() {
    delete health;  // Destructor cleans up memory
  }
};


int main() {
    Monster* goblin = new Monster();  // Dynamically allocated
monster object
    // Forgetting to call delete on goblin causes a memory leak

    return 0;
}
```

In the example above, if we **forget** to delete the goblin object, the memory allocated for its health is never freed, causing a **memory leak**. Always ensure that delete is called for each dynamically allocated object.

3. Profiling and Performance Tools

To ensure your game is running efficiently and not leaking memory, you need to profile and monitor its performance. Profiling tools can help you identify performance bottlenecks and memory usage patterns.

Common Profiling Tools

- **Valgrind (Linux)**: A powerful tool for memory management, Valgrind helps detect **memory leaks, invalid memory accesses**, and **performance bottlenecks**.

- **Visual Studio Profiler (Windows)**: Built into Visual Studio, this tool allows you to track **CPU usage, memory allocation,** and other performance metrics.

- **gprof (Linux/macOS)**: A profiling tool that helps identify function calls and their respective times, useful for optimizing performance.

How to Use Valgrind:

1. **Install Valgrind** (on Linux):

2. sudo apt-get install valgrind

3. **Run your program with Valgrind**:

4. valgrind --leak-check=full ./your_program

5. **Analyze the output**: Valgrind will report memory leaks and invalid memory accesses, helping you pinpoint areas that need fixing.

How to Use Visual Studio Profiler:

1. **Start a performance session**: In Visual Studio, go to **Debug > Performance Profiler**.

2. **Run the game**: Select **CPU Usage, Memory Usage**, or other tools and click on **Start**.

3. **Analyze the results**: After running your game, you'll be able to see graphs and detailed data on **CPU time, memory consumption**, and more.

Hands-On Project: Optimize a Game's Memory-Intensive Functions

Now that you understand the basics of memory management and optimization, let's apply this knowledge to optimize a **game loop** that suffers from **memory leaks** and inefficient memory usage.

Step 1: The Inefficient Game Loop

Imagine we have a simple game loop that creates and destroys **GameObject** instances each frame. This creates a memory bottleneck, as new objects are repeatedly allocated and deallocated without efficient memory management.

```cpp
#include <iostream>
#include <vector>

class GameObject {
public:
    int * data;
    GameObject(int size) {
        data = new int[size]; // Allocate memory
    }
    ~GameObject() {
        delete[] data; // Deallocate memory
    }
};

void gameLoop() {
    std::vector<GameObject *> objects;
```

```
    // Memory-intensive operations: constantly creating and deleting
objects
    for (int i = 0; i < 1000; i++) {
        GameObject * obj = new GameObject(1000);  // Memory
allocation each frame
        objects.push_back(obj);
        delete obj;  // Memory deallocation each frame
    }
}

int main() {
    gameLoop();
    return 0;
}
```

Step 2: Refactor Using Smart Pointers and Memory Pools

Instead of dynamically allocating and deallocating memory each frame, we can use **smart pointers** (specifically std::unique_ptr) to ensure memory is automatically cleaned up when no longer in use. We can also use a **memory pool** to efficiently manage large numbers of game objects.

Refactored Code with Smart Pointers and Memory Pools:

```
#include <iostream>
#include <vector>
#include <memory>
```

```cpp
class GameObject {
public:
    int* data;
    GameObject(int size) {
        data = new int[size]; // Allocate memory
    }
    ~GameObject() {
        delete[] data; // Deallocate memory
    }
};

void gameLoop() {
    std::vector<std::unique_ptr<GameObject>> objects;

    // Use smart pointers to manage memory automatically
    for (int i = 0; i < 1000; i++) {
        objects.push_back(std::make_unique<GameObject>(1000)); // Smart pointer
    }

    // Objects will be automatically cleaned up when they go out of scope
}

int main() {
    gameLoop();
```

return 0;

}

Explanation:

- We use **std::unique_ptr** to manage memory automatically, ensuring that objects are deallocated when they go out of scope.

- The **memory pool** concept can be applied by reusing pre-allocated blocks of memory for large objects. However, the basic idea here is to eliminate unnecessary memory allocation and deallocation by using smart pointers.

Step 3: Performance Testing and Validation

After refactoring the game loop, run your game and profile it using tools like **Valgrind** or **Visual Studio Profiler**. You should see improvements in memory usage, as objects are no longer continuously allocated and freed.

Conclusion

In this chapter, we've covered essential topics for game developers who want to efficiently manage memory and optimize performance:

1. **Manual memory management**: Understanding how to use **pointers** and **dynamic memory** in C++.

2. **Avoiding memory leaks**: Best practices for ensuring memory is properly allocated and deallocated.

3. **Profiling tools**: How to track and optimize your game's memory usage and overall performance.

4. **Hands-on project:** Refactoring a memory-intensive game loop using **smart pointers** and **memory pools** to eliminate memory leaks and optimize performance.

By implementing these techniques in your own games, you can ensure that they run smoothly and efficiently, even as they scale in complexity. In the next chapter, we'll dive deeper into **game systems optimization** and further enhance your understanding of efficient game design.

Chapter 7: Game Engine Fundamentals

Introduction

As you advance in your game development journey, understanding the inner workings of a **game engine** becomes increasingly important. A game engine is a critical component of any video game, providing the essential structure that enables the creation of complex systems and interactive experiences. In this chapter, we will break down the **fundamentals of game engines**, including their role in simplifying game development, how the **game loop** drives performance, and how the **rendering pipeline** transforms your game's graphics into the action you see on-screen.

By the end of this chapter, you will:

1. **Understand the core functions** of a game engine.

2. Gain a deep understanding of the **game loop** and its crucial role in game performance.

3. Learn about **rendering pipelines** and how they render game states and graphics.

4. Build a simple game engine with a **basic game loop** that renders an object on the screen.

Let's dive into the **exciting world** of game engines and see how the underlying mechanics work to power the games we play!

What You'll Need

Before we get started, make sure you have the following tools and setup ready:

Software:

- **IDE (Integrated Development Environment)**: Use **Visual Studio**, **Code::Blocks**, or **CLion**. These are great for handling C++ game development.

- **C++ Compiler**: Ensure your IDE has a C++11 or later compiler. Visual Studio comes preconfigured, and Code::Blocks can be set up with MinGW for C++ development.

- **Graphics Library**: You'll need a graphics library like **SDL2** or **SFML** for rendering. These libraries are lightweight and perfect for building a simple game engine.

- **Profiler**: For testing performance, install a profiler like **gprof** or **Visual Studio Profiler** to track how efficiently your game engine is running.

Hardware:

- A **modern laptop or desktop** with **at least 4GB of RAM** should be sufficient for the simple game engine we're going to build. However, for larger-scale game development, a more powerful system is preferable.

- **Graphics Card**: While basic games can run on integrated graphics, more complex games will require a dedicated GPU for better rendering performance.

1. Understanding Game Engines: What They Are and How They Simplify Development

A **game engine** is a framework or platform that simplifies the creation of games. It provides the building blocks for game developers to create and manage the various aspects of their game, including:

- **Graphics rendering**

- **Physics simulation**

- **Audio management**

- **User input handling**

- **Networking (for multiplayer games)**

Instead of writing all these systems from scratch, game engines provide pre-built solutions to common problems, allowing developers to focus more on creating the **gameplay** and **content** itself.

Core Functions of a Game Engine:

1. **Rendering System**: Handles how graphics are drawn on the screen, including **2D or 3D rendering**.

2. **Physics Engine**: Simulates the physical interactions in the game world, such as collision detection, gravity, and object movement.

3. **Audio System**: Manages sound effects, music, and voice acting.

4. **Input System**: Interprets user input from devices like the mouse, keyboard, or controller.

5. **Game Loop**: The continuous process that runs the game, checking for inputs, updating game states, and rendering the results on-screen.

6. **Scripting**: Many game engines allow you to write game logic in scripting languages like **Lua**, **Python**, or **C#**.

Examples of Popular Game Engines:

- **Unity**: A very popular engine, particularly for indie developers. Unity uses **C#** for scripting.

- **Unreal Engine**: Known for its high-quality graphics and advanced features. Unreal uses **C++** and its own scripting language, **Blueprints**.

- **Godot**: An open-source engine that uses **GDScript** (similar to Python) and **C++**.

- **SFML/SDL2**: Simple game engines that provide a foundation for learning how games work on a basic level.

2. The Game Loop: The Heart of Your Game Engine

At the core of every game is the **game loop**. This loop is responsible for keeping the game running, handling user input, updating the game state, and rendering graphics on the screen. Without the game loop, there would be no game!

What is the Game Loop?

The **game loop** is a continuously running cycle that performs several essential tasks:

1. **Process Input**: Checks for user input (e.g., keyboard, mouse, controller).

2. **Update Game State**: Updates the positions of game objects, checks for collisions, processes AI, etc.

3. **Render Graphics**: Draws everything on the screen.

4. **Repeat**: The loop runs continuously, repeating these tasks until the game is closed.

Basic Game Loop Structure:

```cpp
#include <iostream>
#include <SDL2/SDL.h>

bool isRunning = true;

void gameLoop() {
    while (isRunning) {
        // Step 1: Handle input events
        SDL_Event event;
        while (SDL_PollEvent(&event)) {
            if (event.type == SDL_QUIT) {
                isRunning = false;
            }
        }

        // Step 2: Update game state (e.g., move objects)
        // This will be expanded later
```

```cpp
    // Step 3: Render graphics
    // Clear screen
    SDL_RenderClear(renderer);

    // Render your game objects here

    // Present the screen
    SDL_RenderPresent(renderer);
  }
}

int main() {
  // Initialize SDL
  if (SDL_Init(SDL_INIT_VIDEO) < 0) {
    std::cout << "SDL could not initialize! SDL_Error: " <<
SDL_GetError() << std::endl;
    return -1;
  }


  // Create window
  SDL_Window* window = SDL_CreateWindow("Game Loop
Example", SDL_WINDOWPOS_UNDEFINED,
SDL_WINDOWPOS_UNDEFINED, 800, 600,
SDL_WINDOW_SHOWN);
  if (!window) {
```

```
        std::cout << "Window could not be created! SDL_Error: " <<
SDL_GetError() << std::endl;

        return -1;
    }


    // Create renderer
    SDL_Renderer* renderer = SDL_CreateRenderer(window, -1,
SDL_RENDERER_ACCELERATED);


    // Run the game loop
    gameLoop();


    // Clean up and quit SDL
    SDL_DestroyRenderer(renderer);
    SDL_DestroyWindow(window);
    SDL_Quit();


    return 0;
}
```

Explanation:

- The game loop continuously checks for events (SDL_PollEvent) to handle input, updates the game state, and then renders the game state to the screen.

- **SDL_RenderClear()** clears the screen for the next frame, and **SDL_RenderPresent()** presents the rendered frame.

Why the Game Loop is Essential

- The game loop is the foundation of all **real-time systems**. Without it, your game would be static and would not respond to user input or update the game state dynamically.

- **Performance**: The efficiency of the game loop is critical for smooth gameplay. Optimizing how the game loop processes updates and renders graphics will directly impact the frame rate and performance of your game.

3. Rendering Pipelines: How Graphics Are Rendered

The **rendering pipeline** is the process that takes data (game objects, textures, shaders, etc.) and converts it into images on the screen. This process is what makes your game **visually interactive**.

Graphics Pipeline Overview

The pipeline can be broken down into several stages:

1. **Vertex Processing**: The vertices (points) of a 3D model are transformed from object space to screen space.

2. **Clipping**: Objects outside the view are discarded.

3. **Rasterization**: The 2D image is drawn from the 3D data.

4. **Fragment Processing**: Pixels are shaded and textures are applied.

5. **Frame Buffer**: The final image is displayed on the screen.

2D vs 3D Rendering

- **2D Rendering**: This is simpler, and involves drawing objects (sprites, UI elements, etc.) directly on the screen. **SDL2** or **SFML** handles this with ease.

- **3D Rendering**: This is more complex, as it involves transforming 3D objects into a 2D projection on the screen. Libraries like **OpenGL** or **DirectX** handle 3D rendering.

Using SDL2 or SFML for Rendering

Both **SDL2** and **SFML** offer easy-to-use systems for handling 2D graphics and rendering. Let's take a closer look at a basic example using **SDL2** to render an object.

Rendering an Object Using SDL2:

```
#include <SDL2/SDL.h>


SDL_Renderer* renderer;


void renderObject() {
    // Draw a rectangle on the screen
    SDL_Rect rect = {100, 100, 50, 50}; // x, y, width, height
    SDL_SetRenderDrawColor(renderer, 255, 0, 0, 255); // Red color
    SDL_RenderFillRect(renderer, &rect); // Fill the rectangle
    SDL_RenderPresent(renderer); // Show the updated content
}


int main() {
```

```cpp
SDL_Init(SDL_INIT_VIDEO);

SDL_Window* window = SDL_CreateWindow("Rendering
Example", SDL_WINDOWPOS_UNDEFINED,
SDL_WINDOWPOS_UNDEFINED, 800, 600,
SDL_WINDOW_SHOWN);

renderer = SDL_CreateRenderer(window, -1,
SDL_RENDERER_ACCELERATED);

bool isRunning = true;
SDL_Event event;
while (isRunning) {
    while (SDL_PollEvent(&event)) {
        if (event.type == SDL_QUIT) {
            isRunning = false;
        }
    }

    SDL_RenderClear(renderer);  // Clear screen before drawing
    renderObject();  // Render the object
}

SDL_DestroyRenderer(renderer);
SDL_DestroyWindow(window);
SDL_Quit();
return 0;
}
```

Explanation:

- **SDL_RenderDrawColor** sets the drawing color for objects.

- **SDL_RenderFillRect** draws a solid red rectangle.

- **SDL_RenderPresent** updates the window to show the newly rendered content.

---

4. Hands-On Project: Build a Simple Game Engine with a Basic Game Loop

In this project, we'll build a simple **game engine** with a basic **game loop** and rendering functionality. Our engine will create a window, enter a game loop, and render a simple object (a rectangle) on the screen.

Step 1: Setup the Game Window

We'll use **SDL2** to create the window and set up the game loop. This loop will check for user input, update the game state, and render the object on the screen.

```cpp
#include <SDL2/SDL.h>
#include <iostream>

SDL_Window* window;
SDL_Renderer* renderer;

bool init() {
    if (SDL_Init(SDL_INIT_VIDEO) < 0) {
        std::cout << "SDL could not initialize! SDL_Error: " << SDL_GetError() << std::endl;
        return false;
```

```
    }
    window = SDL_CreateWindow("Simple Game Engine",
SDL_WINDOWPOS_UNDEFINED,
SDL_WINDOWPOS_UNDEFINED, 800, 600,
SDL_WINDOW_SHOWN);
    if (!window) {
        std::cout << "Window could not be created! SDL_Error: " <<
SDL_GetError() << std::endl;
        return false;
    }
    renderer = SDL_CreateRenderer(window, -1,
SDL_RENDERER_ACCELERATED);
    return true;
}


void render() {
    SDL_RenderClear(renderer);


    SDL_Rect rect = {300, 200, 100, 100};  // Position and size of the
rectangle
    SDL_SetRenderDrawColor(renderer, 255, 0, 0, 255);  // Red
color
    SDL_RenderFillRect(renderer, &rect);


    SDL_RenderPresent(renderer);
}


void close() {
```

```cpp
    SDL_DestroyRenderer(renderer);
    SDL_DestroyWindow(window);
    SDL_Quit();
}

int main() {
    if (!init()) {
        std::cout << "Initialization failed!" << std::endl;
        return -1;
    }

    bool isRunning = true;
    SDL_Event e;

    while (isRunning) {
        while (SDL_PollEvent(&e) != 0) {
            if (e.type == SDL_QUIT) {
                isRunning = false;
            }
        }

        render();
    }

    close();
```

return 0;

}

Step 2: Explanation of the Game Engine

1. **Initialization (init):**

   o   We initialize **SDL2** and create the **game window** and **renderer.**

   o   The **renderer** is used for drawing everything on the screen.

2. **Rendering (render):**

   o   We clear the screen and draw a red rectangle at a fixed position. The rectangle is filled and displayed using SDL_RenderPresent.

3. **Closing the Engine (close):**

   o   We properly clean up resources by destroying the renderer and window before quitting SDL.

Conclusion

In this chapter, we:

1. Explored the core functions of **game engines** and their role in simplifying game development.

2. Dissected the **game loop** and its critical role in managing input, updates, and rendering in real-time systems.

3. Learned about the **rendering pipeline**, from vertex processing to pixel shading.

4. Built a simple **game engine** with a basic **game loop** and rendering functionality using **SDL2**.

This foundational knowledge sets the stage for building more complex game engines or working with existing ones like **Unity** or **Unreal Engine**. By understanding the low-level mechanics of a game engine, you'll be able to make better decisions about how to manage game states, optimize performance, and integrate complex systems like **physics** and **AI**.

Chapter 8: Graphics and Rendering in C++

Introduction to 2D and 3D Graphics

Graphics rendering is a cornerstone of modern game development. The ability to display visual content effectively, efficiently, and interactively is essential to creating compelling games. In this chapter, we'll dive into the basics of rendering graphics in C++ using libraries like **OpenGL** and **DirectX**, covering both **2D and 3D graphics**. We will also look at **shaders**, which play a vital role in the rendering pipeline, and **game assets** like textures and models, which bring your game world to life.

By the end of this chapter, you'll be able to:

1. Understand the basic concepts of **2D and 3D graphics rendering**.

2. Work with **shaders** and **GPU programming** to enhance your game's visuals.

3. Learn how to handle **game assets**, including loading and displaying textures, models, and other media.

4. Create a simple 2D sprite renderer using **OpenGL**.

Let's explore how rendering works in C++ and how you can use it to create vibrant, interactive game environments!

What You'll Need

Before we get started with the concepts and code, let's make sure you have the necessary tools and setup:

Software:

- **IDE (Integrated Development Environment):** You can use **Visual Studio, CLion,** or **Code::Blocks** for C++ development. Visual Studio is recommended because it integrates seamlessly with OpenGL and DirectX.

- **OpenGL:** For 2D and 3D graphics rendering, we will primarily use **OpenGL.** It's cross-platform and widely used in the industry. You'll also need libraries like **GLFW** (for window/context management) and **GLEW** (for OpenGL extensions).

- **GLFW and GLEW:** These libraries help set up an OpenGL context and load OpenGL functions respectively. You can install these libraries via package managers or manually from their websites.

- **Graphics Card:** A **dedicated graphics card** (NVIDIA, AMD, etc.) will be essential for rendering complex graphics. For basic 2D graphics, integrated graphics may suffice.

Hardware:

- **4GB of RAM or more:** For handling graphics and running the game engine smoothly.

- **Modern CPU:** A dual-core processor or better will help with rendering and processing the game loop efficiently.

- **Graphics Card (GPU):** While basic games can run with integrated graphics, for 3D games and advanced rendering, a dedicated GPU will significantly improve performance.

1. Introduction to 2D and 3D Graphics

Graphics rendering can be broadly divided into **2D** and **3D graphics**:

2D Graphics

2D graphics involve rendering images (or sprites) in a flat, two-dimensional space. Games that use 2D graphics typically feature a **side-scrolling view**, **top-down view**, or **isometric perspective**. Examples include platformers, puzzle games, and top-down shooters.

3D Graphics

3D graphics, on the other hand, are rendered in a three-dimensional space. These games involve **3D models**, lighting effects, **textures**, and **camera perspectives**. Examples include first-person shooters, role-playing games (RPGs), and racing games.

In both 2D and 3D, rendering involves transforming game objects and their properties (position, color, texture, etc.) into a visual representation on the screen.

How Graphics Rendering Works

Graphics rendering works through the **Graphics Pipeline**, which processes the game world into pixels that are displayed on the screen. This process typically involves:

1. **Vertex Processing**: The position and properties of each vertex (point) of 3D models are processed.

2. **Transformation**: Vertices are transformed from **object space** to **screen space**.

3. **Clipping**: Objects outside of the camera view are discarded.

4. **Rasterization**: The 3D data is converted into 2D pixels.

5. **Fragment Processing**: Each pixel is colored, shaded, and textured.

6. **Display**: The final image is displayed on the screen.

---

2. Working with Shaders and GPU Programming

What Are Shaders?

A **shader** is a small program that runs on the GPU (Graphics Processing Unit) and defines how graphics are rendered. There are several types of shaders, but the most common are **vertex shaders** and **fragment (or pixel) shaders**:

- **Vertex Shaders**: Handle the processing of vertex data (e.g., the position of a 3D model's vertices) and apply transformations like rotation, scaling, and translation.

- **Fragment Shaders**: Handle the coloring and texturing of pixels on the screen. They calculate the final color of each pixel, applying effects like lighting, shadows, and textures.

Shaders are written in a **shader programming language** such as **GLSL** (OpenGL Shading Language) for OpenGL, or **HLSL** for DirectX. In OpenGL, shaders are executed in parallel on the GPU, making them extremely efficient for real-time rendering.

How Shaders Work in OpenGL

Here's a basic example of a vertex and fragment shader written in GLSL:

Vertex Shader (vertex_shader.glsl):

#version 330 core

```
layout(location = 0) in vec3 aPos; // Vertex position
layout(location = 1) in vec3 aColor; // Vertex color

out vec3 ourColor; // Output color to fragment shader

uniform mat4 model;
uniform mat4 view;
uniform mat4 projection;

void main() {
    gl_Position = projection * view * model * vec4(aPos, 1.0); //
Apply transformations
    ourColor = aColor; // Pass color to fragment shader
}
```

Fragment Shader (fragment_shader.glsl):

```
#version 330 core
out vec4 FragColor; // Output color of the fragment

in vec3 ourColor; // Input color from vertex shader

void main() {
    FragColor = vec4(ourColor, 1.0); // Set the pixel color
}
```

Explanation:

- The **vertex shader** transforms the position of vertices and passes the color to the **fragment shader**.

- The **fragment shader** sets the pixel color based on the passed input color.

---

3. Loading and Handling Game Assets

For a game to feel alive, it needs **assets**—textures, models, sounds, etc. Loading and managing these assets efficiently is essential for game performance.

Textures

Textures are images applied to game objects (3D models or 2D sprites). A texture can be a simple image or a more complex **normal map** or **bump map** used for adding depth to 3D surfaces.

In **OpenGL**, textures are typically loaded into the GPU using **texture objects**. Here's an example of how to load a texture:

```
GLuint loadTexture(const char* path) {
    GLuint textureID;
    glGenTextures(1, &textureID);
    glBindTexture(GL_TEXTURE_2D, textureID);

    // Load image
    int width, height, nrChannels;
    stbi_set_flip_vertically_on_load(true); // Flip image for correct orientation
    unsigned char *data = stbi_load(path, &width, &height, &nrChannels, 0);

    if (data) {
```

```
    // Generate the texture

    glTexImage2D(GL_TEXTURE_2D, 0, GL_RGB, width,
height, 0, GL_RGB, GL_UNSIGNED_BYTE, data);

    glGenerateMipmap(GL_TEXTURE_2D);

  } else {

    std::cout << "Failed to load texture!" << std::endl;

  }


  stbi_image_free(data);

  return textureID;

}
```

Models

In 3D games, models are complex objects made up of vertices, edges, and faces. **Meshes** represent these models, and they are typically loaded from file formats like **OBJ**, **FBX**, or **GLTF**.

// Code for loading models typically involves reading file formats

// and storing vertex data, normals, texture coordinates, etc.

---

4. Hands-On Project: Rendering a Simple 2D Sprite Using OpenGL

Now that we have an understanding of the basics of graphics, rendering, and shaders, let's create a simple OpenGL application to render a **2D sprite** on the screen. We'll create a **window**, load a **texture**, and render a **rectangle** (sprite) with the texture applied.

Step 1: Setting Up OpenGL with GLFW and GLEW

To set up OpenGL, we'll use **GLFW** for window/context management and **GLEW** for managing OpenGL extensions.

1. **Install GLFW and GLEW** (using package managers or manual installation).

2. Link the libraries in your IDE project.

Step 2: Basic OpenGL Setup

```cpp
#include <GLFW/glfw3.h>
#include <GL/glew.h>
#include <iostream>

int main() {
    // Initialize GLFW
    if (!glfwInit()) {
        std::cout << "Failed to initialize GLFW!" << std::endl;
        return -1;
    }

    // Create a windowed OpenGL window
    GLFWwindow* window = glfwCreateWindow(800, 600, "2D Sprite Rendering", nullptr, nullptr);
    if (!window) {
        std::cout << "Failed to create GLFW window!" << std::endl;
        glfwTerminate();
        return -1;
    }
```

```cpp
// Make the window's context current
glfwMakeContextCurrent(window);
glfwSetFramebufferSizeCallback(window,
framebuffer_size_callback);

// Initialize GLEW
if (glewInit() != GLEW_OK) {
    std::cout << "Failed to initialize GLEW!" << std::endl;
    return -1;
}

// Game loop
while (!glfwWindowShouldClose(window)) {
    // Clear the screen with a color
    glClearColor(0.1f, 0.1f, 0.1f, 1.0f); // Dark background
    glClear(GL_COLOR_BUFFER_BIT);

    // Render your game objects here (e.g., a sprite)

    // Swap buffers
    glfwSwapBuffers(window);
    glfwPollEvents();
}

glfwTerminate();
```

return 0;

}

Step 3: Loading a Texture and Applying It to a Quad

Now, we'll load a texture (such as a simple image) and apply it to a **quad** (rectangle).

```
GLuint loadTexture(const char* path) {
    // Load the texture from the file
    GLuint textureID;
    glGenTextures(1, &textureID);
    glBindTexture(GL_TEXTURE_2D, textureID);

    int width, height, nrChannels;
    unsigned char *data = stbi_load(path, &width, &height, &nrChannels, 0);
    if (data) {
        glTexImage2D(GL_TEXTURE_2D, 0, GL_RGB, width, height, 0, GL_RGB, GL_UNSIGNED_BYTE, data);
        glGenerateMipmap(GL_TEXTURE_2D);
    } else {
        std::cout << "Failed to load texture!" << std::endl;
    }

    stbi_image_free(data);
    return textureID;
}
```

You can now render the **texture** onto a quad (rectangle) and display it.

Step 4: Rendering the Sprite

To render the sprite, you will need a shader to apply the texture, and a **VAO** (Vertex Array Object) and **VBO** (Vertex Buffer Object) to handle the quad's vertices.

// Create and compile shaders, load vertex data (quad), apply texture

After following these steps, your game will render a simple 2D sprite on the screen using OpenGL.

Conclusion

In this chapter, we've learned about:

1. **2D and 3D graphics rendering**, including how graphics are processed and displayed on the screen.

2. **Shaders** and **GPU programming**, including how vertex and fragment shaders work to manipulate graphics data.

3. How to load and manage **game assets** like textures and models to bring your game to life.

4. A hands-on project where we built a simple OpenGL-based renderer to display a 2D sprite.

With this foundational knowledge, you can now start creating richer and more interactive visual experiences in your games. The concepts of graphics and rendering are just the beginning—there's much more to explore in terms of **lighting**, **shaders**, and **3D models**, which we will dive into in future chapters.

Chapter 9: Physics and Collision Detection

Introduction to Physics and Collision Detection in Games

One of the most exciting aspects of game development is making the world come alive with **realistic physics** and interactions. The ability to simulate the **movement** of objects, their response to forces, and how they **collide** with each other adds depth and immersion to any game. Whether it's a **2D platformer**, a **3D racing game**, or an **action-adventure** game, **physics engines** and **collision detection** are fundamental components.

In this chapter, we will explore the following topics:

1. **Physics engines** and how they simulate real-world movement and forces.

2. **Collision detection algorithms**, including **Axis-Aligned Bounding Box (AABB)** and **circle collisions**, along with optimizations to enhance performance.

3. A **hands-on project** where we will create a **basic physics simulation** with **collision detection** in a **2D environment**.

By the end of this chapter, you'll be equipped to implement simple physics simulations and collision detection systems in your own games.

What You'll Need

Before diving into the technical details, let's ensure you have the right tools to follow along:

Software:

- **IDE (Integrated Development Environment)**: A good C++ IDE like **Visual Studio**, **Code::Blocks**, or **CLion** will work well.

- **C++ Compiler**: Make sure your IDE is set up with a C++11 or later compiler.

- **Physics Library (Optional)**: While we'll be building a simple physics system from scratch, libraries like **Box2D** or **Chipmunk** are available if you wish to integrate more advanced physics systems later.

- **Graphics Library**: **SFML** or **SDL2** is required for rendering 2D shapes and handling window creation. This is important for visualizing the physics and collisions.

Hardware:

- A **laptop or desktop** with **4GB of RAM** should suffice for this chapter. More complex physics simulations may require more resources, but for now, this setup is enough.

- A **graphics card** is not essential for simple 2D physics simulations, but a dedicated GPU is required for 3D physics in more complex scenarios.

1. Physics Engines: Introduction to Physics in Games

A **physics engine** simulates the physical world inside your game, giving objects realistic properties like **gravity, velocity, friction**, and **acceleration**. Physics engines help make the interaction between objects in your game feel natural, simulating things like the **fall of an object, character movements**, and how objects **collide** with each other.

Physics engines are typically used for two main tasks:

1. **Rigid body dynamics**: Simulating the movement of solid objects that don't deform upon collision (e.g., a box, a ball, or a car).

2. **Soft body dynamics**: Simulating deformable objects, such as cloth or liquids.

In this chapter, we'll focus on **rigid body dynamics** for our 2D physics simulation.

Key Concepts of Game Physics

1. **Velocity**: The speed and direction of an object.

2. **Acceleration**: The rate of change of velocity.

3. **Gravity**: A force that pulls objects down toward the ground.

4. **Friction**: The resistance that occurs when two objects move against each other.

These principles help simulate how objects move, collide, and interact within the game world.

2. Collision Detection Algorithms

Collision detection is the process of determining whether two objects in the game world intersect or come into contact. The goal of collision detection is to handle interactions between objects, such as when a character walks into a wall or when two balls collide.

There are several types of collision detection algorithms, and we'll focus on two common ones used in games:

1. **Axis-Aligned Bounding Box (AABB)**:

    o   This algorithm uses **rectangular boxes** to represent the bounds of objects.

    o   The boxes are "aligned" along the axes of the coordinate system, meaning they don't rotate.

2. **Circle Collision**:

    o   This algorithm uses **circles** to represent objects and checks if two circles are touching or overlapping.

1. Axis-Aligned Bounding Box (AABB)

AABB uses simple rectangular boxes to define the boundary of an object. The algorithm checks if two boxes **overlap** on the X and Y axes.

AABB Collision Detection

Here's the basic algorithm:

1. Check if the **x** coordinates of the boxes overlap.

2. Check if the **y** coordinates of the boxes overlap.

3. If both conditions are true, then the boxes are colliding.

Example Code for AABB Collision Detection:

```cpp
#include <iostream>

struct AABB {
    float x, y, width, height; // x, y is the position; width, height are the dimensions
};

bool checkCollision(const AABB& box1, const AABB& box2) {
    return (box1.x < box2.x + box2.width && box1.x + box1.width > box2.x &&
            box1.y < box2.y + box2.height && box1.y + box1.height > box2.y);
}

int main() {
    AABB box1 = {0, 0, 50, 50}; // Box 1: positioned at (0, 0) with a width and height of 50
    AABB box2 = {25, 25, 50, 50}; // Box 2: positioned at (25, 25) with a width and height of 50

    if (checkCollision(box1, box2)) {
        std::cout << "Collision detected!" << std::endl;
    } else {
        std::cout << "No collision." << std::endl;
    }
```

```
    return 0;
}
```

Explanation:

- **checkCollision()** checks if the **two AABBs overlap** on both the **x-axis** and **y-axis**.

- This is the most common form of collision detection used in **2D games**, as it's fast and simple.

2. Circle Collision

Circle collision detection is used for objects that are represented as circles, like balls or circular characters. The algorithm checks if the distance between the centers of two circles is less than the sum of their radii.

Circle Collision Detection

1. Calculate the **distance** between the centers of the two circles.

2. Compare the distance to the sum of their **radii**.

3. If the distance is less than the sum of their radii, then the circles are colliding.

Example Code for Circle Collision Detection:

```cpp
#include <iostream>
#include <cmath>

struct Circle {
    float x, y, radius; // x, y is the position; radius is the size
};
```

```cpp
bool checkCollision(const Circle& circle1, const Circle& circle2) {
    float dx = circle1.x - circle2.x;
    float dy = circle1.y - circle2.y;
    float distance = std::sqrt(dx * dx + dy * dy);
    return distance < (circle1.radius + circle2.radius);
}

int main() {
    Circle circle1 = {0, 0, 30}; // Circle 1: positioned at (0, 0) with a radius of 30
    Circle circle2 = {25, 25, 30}; // Circle 2: positioned at (25, 25) with a radius of 30

    if (checkCollision(circle1, circle2)) {
        std::cout << "Collision detected!" << std::endl;
    } else {
        std::cout << "No collision." << std::endl;
    }

    return 0;
}
```

Explanation:

- The **distance** between the centers of the circles is calculated using the **Euclidean distance formula.**

- The circles collide if the distance between their centers is less than the sum of their **radii**.

---

3. Hands-On Project: Create a Basic Physics Simulation with Collision Detection in 2D

Now that we've covered collision detection, let's put everything into practice by creating a **simple 2D physics simulation**. We'll simulate basic physics with gravity, velocity, and **collision detection** using the AABB algorithm.

Step 1: Setting Up the Game Loop

We will create a basic **game loop** that:

- Processes input.
- Updates the positions of objects based on **velocity** and **gravity**.
- Checks for **collisions** using the **AABB** algorithm.
- Renders the objects to the screen using **SDL2** for simplicity.

Code for the Game Loop:

```cpp
#include <iostream>
#include <SDL2/SDL.h>

struct AABB {
    float x, y, width, height;
    float velocityX, velocityY;
};
```

```
bool checkCollision(const AABB& box1, const AABB& box2) {
    return (box1.x < box2.x + box2.width && box1.x + box1.width >
box2.x &&
            box1.y < box2.y + box2.height && box1.y + box1.height >
box2.y);
}


void update(AABB& box, float deltaTime) {
    // Apply gravity
    box.velocityY += 9.81f * deltaTime;

    // Update position based on velocity
    box.x += box.velocityX * deltaTime;
    box.y += box.velocityY * deltaTime;

    // Simple floor collision detection (bounce off the ground)
    if (box.y + box.height > 600) {
        box.y = 600 - box.height; // Reset position to ground level
        box.velocityY = -box.velocityY * 0.8f; // Reflect velocity with
some damping
    }
}


void render(SDL_Renderer* renderer, const AABB& box) {
    SDL_Rect rect = {static_cast<int>(box.x), static_cast<int>(box.y),
static_cast<int>(box.width), static_cast<int>(box.height)};
```

```cpp
    SDL_SetRenderDrawColor(renderer, 255, 0, 0, 255); // Red
color
    SDL_RenderFillRect(renderer, &rect);
}


int main() {
    if (SDL_Init(SDL_INIT_VIDEO) < 0) {
        std::cout << "SDL could not initialize! SDL_Error: " <<
SDL_GetError() << std::endl;
        return -1;
    }


    SDL_Window* window = SDL_CreateWindow("Physics
Simulation", SDL_WINDOWPOS_UNDEFINED,
SDL_WINDOWPOS_UNDEFINED, 800, 600,
SDL_WINDOW_SHOWN);
    SDL_Renderer* renderer = SDL_CreateRenderer(window, -1,
SDL_RENDERER_ACCELERATED);


    AABB box = {100, 100, 50, 50, 0, 0}; // Start at (100,100) with a
size of 50x50


    bool isRunning = true;
    SDL_Event event;
    Uint32 lastTime = SDL_GetTicks();


    while (isRunning) {
        Uint32 currentTime = SDL_GetTicks();
```

```
    float deltaTime = (currentTime - lastTime) / 1000.0f; //
Calculate deltaTime in seconds
    lastTime = currentTime;

    while (SDL_PollEvent(&event)) {
      if (event.type == SDL_QUIT) {
        isRunning = false;
      }
    }

    // Update physics
    update(box, deltaTime);

    // Render
    SDL_RenderClear(renderer);
    render(renderer, box);
    SDL_RenderPresent(renderer);

    SDL_Delay(16); // Simple frame cap (~60 FPS)
  }

  SDL_DestroyRenderer(renderer);
  SDL_DestroyWindow(window);
  SDL_Quit();

  return 0;
```

/

Step 2: Explanation of the Code

1. **Game Loop**: We run the game loop, where we:

   o Process user input.

   o Update the physics of the game objects (in this case, a **falling box** with gravity).

   o Render the box on the screen.

2. **Physics Update**: The object's **velocity** is updated based on gravity, and the **position** is updated based on the current velocity. We check for collisions with the floor, and if the box hits the ground, it **bounces**.

3. **Rendering**: The box is rendered as a **red rectangle** on the screen.

Step 3: Running the Simulation

After running the program, you should see a red box falling under gravity. When it hits the ground, it will bounce slightly, simulating basic physics with **velocity, gravity**, and **collision detection**.

Conclusion

In this chapter, we:

1. Explored the basics of **physics engines** and their role in creating realistic movement and interactions.

2. Learned how to implement **collision detection** algorithms like **AABB** and **circle collisions**.

3. Built a simple 2D physics simulation that includes **gravity, velocity**, and **collision detection**.

4. Used **SDL2** to render objects and simulate real-time physics in the game loop.

Physics and collision detection are foundational to building interactive, immersive games. As you continue developing your game, these systems will evolve to handle more complex interactions, such as **3D physics**, **rigid body dynamics**, and **advanced collision algorithms**.

Chapter 10: Artificial Intelligence in Games

Introduction to Artificial Intelligence in Game Development

Artificial Intelligence (AI) is a core component of modern games, allowing **enemies**, **NPCs (Non-Player Characters)**, and even the **game world itself** to react and adapt to the player's actions. From simple decision-making mechanisms to complex systems that simulate human-like behavior, AI is responsible for making games feel alive and interactive.

In this chapter, we will:

1. Explore the basics of AI in games, including techniques like **decision trees**, **state machines**, and **pathfinding algorithms**.

2. Understand how AI is used to control **enemies**, **NPCs**, and **player behaviors**.

3. Implement a **simple AI pathfinding algorithm** using **A***, one of the most commonly used pathfinding algorithms in games.

By the end of this chapter, you will have the foundational knowledge of AI techniques commonly used in games and hands-on experience with an **A*** pathfinding implementation.

What You'll Need

To get started, here are the tools and software you'll need to follow along with the chapter:

Software:

- **IDE (Integrated Development Environment):** Use **Visual Studio, CLion,** or **Code::Blocks.** These are ideal for C++ game development.

- **C++ Compiler:** Make sure your IDE is set up with a C++11 or later compiler. Visual Studio comes preconfigured, and Code::Blocks can be set up with MinGW for C++ development.

- **Graphics Library:** For this chapter, we will use **SDL2** or **SFML** for rendering and handling window management.

- **Pathfinding Visualization Tool** (Optional): If you wish to visualize the A* pathfinding algorithm and its behavior, **SFML** or **SDL2** can help render grid layouts and paths.

Hardware:

- A **laptop or desktop** with at least **4GB of RAM** and a **dual-core processor** should be sufficient for the code examples in this chapter.

- For more complex pathfinding and AI systems, a more powerful computer will be useful, but it's not necessary for the basics we will cover here.

1. AI Basics for Games

In games, **Artificial Intelligence (AI)** refers to the algorithms and systems that control the actions and behaviors of game characters and elements. There are different AI techniques used to create game behaviors, from simple **decision trees** to more complex systems like **state machines** and **pathfinding algorithms**.

1.1 Decision Trees

A **decision tree** is a flowchart-like structure used to make decisions based on certain conditions. Each node of the tree represents a decision point, and the tree branches out based on possible choices or actions.

In games, decision trees are often used to control NPC behavior. For example, a non-playable character (NPC) may choose to **chase** the player, **attack**, or **flee** depending on certain conditions.

Example of a Decision Tree for NPC Behavior:

Is player in range?

   / \

Yes No

  / \

Chase Wander

In this simple decision tree:

- The NPC checks if the player is within a certain range.
- If **yes**, it chases the player.
- If **no**, it starts wandering around the environment.

1.2 State Machines

A **state machine** is another way to handle decisions in AI. It is often used for controlling an NPC's **states** or **modes**, such as **patrolling**, **attacking**, or **fleeing**. The NPC switches between these states based on certain triggers or conditions.

Example of an NPC State Machine:

State: Patrolling

- If player detected: Switch to Attacking

- If health < 20: Switch to Fleeing

The state machine allows the NPC to react dynamically to the game environment, and you can easily add more states and transitions as needed.

1.3 Pathfinding Algorithms

One of the most important aspects of AI is allowing characters to **navigate** through the game world. This is where **pathfinding algorithms** come in. Pathfinding allows NPCs to find the best route from one point to another, avoiding obstacles and navigating the game environment.

The A (A-Star) Algorithm*

A* is one of the most popular and widely used **pathfinding algorithms** in games. It combines the benefits of **Dijkstra's Algorithm** (finding the shortest path) and **Greedy Best-First Search** (finding the fastest path) to efficiently calculate the optimal path.

A* uses the concept of a **cost function** that evaluates the **distance** to the target and the **distance traveled** so far. The two main components are:

- **G(n)**: The cost of the path from the start node to node **n**.

- **H(n)**: The estimated cost to reach the goal node from node **n**.

The formula to calculate the total cost **F(n)** is:

F(n) = G(n) + H(n)

*A Algorithm Steps:**

1. **Start**: Add the start node to an open list.

2. **Loop**: While there are nodes in the open list:

   - Find the node with the lowest **F(n)** value.

   - If it's the target node, we've found the path.

   - Otherwise, generate its neighbors, calculate their **G**, **H**, and **F** values, and add them to the open list.

3. **Goal**: Once the target node is reached, reconstruct the path.

A* is efficient because it uses **heuristics** (estimated distances) to guide its search, making it faster than brute force algorithms like Dijkstra's.

---

2. AI in Game Development: Enemies, NPCs, and Player Behaviors

AI is crucial for creating **interactive gameplay**. From controlling the **movement of enemies** to **NPC dialogues** and **decision-making**, AI makes the game world feel **alive** and **reactive**. In this section, we will focus on how AI is used to control various aspects of gameplay, such as **enemy AI**, **NPC behaviors**, and how AI affects **player interactions**.

2.1 AI for Enemies

Enemy AI in games typically involves deciding how an enemy reacts to the player's actions. Enemies can have simple AI behaviors, such as **chasing, attacking,** or **fleeing.** More complex AI systems involve tactics like **group coordination** and **advanced strategies.**

Example of Simple Enemy AI Behavior:

1. If the player is detected, the enemy **chases** the player.

2. If the player gets too close, the enemy **attacks.**

3. If the enemy's health is low, the enemy **flee.**

2.2 NPC Behavior and Dialogue

NPCs (non-playable characters) in games require AI systems to handle their **behavior,** such as wandering around the game world or interacting with the player. A simple NPC might only have a few behaviors like **walking, sitting,** or **standing.** More complex NPCs may have **dialogue trees** and can **respond** to player actions with dynamic conversations.

Example of NPC AI Behavior:

- **Patrolling**: The NPC moves along a set path and reacts to the player's proximity.

- **Quest Giving**: The NPC gives the player tasks or quests based on their progress in the game.

2.3 Player Behavior

Player AI doesn't refer to the **player** but rather to the **AI systems that mimic player-like behaviors.** This includes tactics like **predicting player movements,** creating **adaptive AI systems** that learn from the player's strategies, or implementing **artificially intelligent opponents** in single-player games.

3. Hands-On Project: Implementing A Pathfinding in a 2D Environment*

Now that we've explored the theory behind AI in games, it's time to dive into a **hands-on project**. In this project, we will implement a **pathfinding algorithm** using **A*** in a **2D environment**. Our goal is to allow an NPC to move from one point to another while avoiding obstacles.

Step 1: Setting Up the Environment

We'll use **SFML** for rendering and handling the window management. SFML is simple, lightweight, and easy to set up for 2D games.

```cpp
#include <SFML/Graphics.hpp>
#include <iostream>
#include <vector>
#include <queue>

struct Node {
    int x, y;
    float gCost, hCost, fCost;
    Node* parent;

    Node(int _x, int _y) : x(_x), y(_y), gCost(0), hCost(0), fCost(0), parent(nullptr) {}

    float getFCost() const { return gCost + hCost; }
};
```

```
bool operator>(const Node& a, const Node& b) {
    return a.getFCost() > b.getFCost();
}
```

Step 2: Implementing the A Algorithm*

We'll implement the A* algorithm to find the shortest path between two points while avoiding obstacles.

```
std::vector<Node *> getNeighbors(Node * current,
std::vector<std::vector<Node>>& grid) {
    std::vector<Node *> neighbors;
    int dirs[4][2] = {{0, 1}, {1, 0}, {0, -1}, {-1, 0}};
    for (auto& dir : dirs) {
        int nx = current->x + dir[0];
        int ny = current->y + dir[1];
        if (nx >= 0 && ny >= 0 && nx < grid.size() && ny <
grid[0].size()) {
            neighbors.push_back(&grid[nx][ny]);
        }
    }
    return neighbors;
}


std::vector<Node *> aStar(Node * start, Node * end,
std::vector<std::vector<Node>>& grid) {
    std::priority_queue<Node *, std::vector<Node *>,
std::greater<Node *>> openSet;
    openSet.push(start);
```

```cpp
std::vector<Node*> path;

while (!openSet.empty()) {
    Node* current = openSet.top();
    openSet.pop();

    if (current == end) {
        while (current != nullptr) {
            path.push_back(current);
            current = current->parent;
        }
        break;
    }

    for (Node* neighbor : getNeighbors(current, grid)) {
        float tentativeGCost = current->gCost + 1;

        if (tentativeGCost < neighbor->gCost) {
            neighbor->parent = current;
            neighbor->gCost = tentativeGCost;
            neighbor->hCost = abs(neighbor->x - end->x) +
abs(neighbor->y - end->y);

            openSet.push(neighbor);
        }
    }
```

```
    }

    return path;
}
```

Step 3: Rendering the Path

Now we'll render the pathfinding solution onto the screen.

```
int main() {
    sf::RenderWindow window(sf::VideoMode(800, 600),
    "Pathfinding with A *");

    std::vector<std::vector<Node>> grid(20, std::vector<Node>(15));

    for (int i = 0; i < 20; ++i) {
        for (int j = 0; j < 15; ++j) {
            grid[i][j] = Node(i, j);
        }
    }

    Node * start = &grid[0][0];
    Node * end = &grid[19][14];

    std::vector<Node *> path = aStar(start, end, grid);

    // Render grid
    while (window.isOpen()) {
        sf::Event event;
```

```
while (window.pollEvent(event)) {
    if (event.type == sf::Event::Closed)
        window.close();
}


window.clear();
// Draw the grid, the path, and the start/end points
for (auto node : path) {
    sf::RectangleShape rect(sf::Vector2f(40.f, 40.f));
    rect.setFillColor(sf::Color::Green);
    rect.setPosition(node->x * 40.f, node->y * 40.f);
    window.draw(rect);
}
window.display();
}


return 0;
}
```

Step 4: Explanation

- **Grid Setup**: We create a grid of nodes, where each node represents a cell in the game world.

- *A Algorithm**: We implement the A* algorithm to calculate the shortest path from the start to the end node.

- **Rendering**: The path is drawn as green squares on the screen.

Conclusion

In this chapter, we:

1. Explored the basics of **AI techniques** used in games, including **decision trees, state machines**, and **pathfinding algorithms**.

2. Learned how AI is used for **enemies, NPCs**, and **player behaviors** to make games more interactive and dynamic.

3. Implemented a hands-on project to create a simple **A*** pathfinding algorithm in a **2D environment**, allowing NPCs to navigate through a grid.

AI is a powerful tool that can significantly enhance gameplay and make games feel more responsive and intelligent. As you continue developing your games, you can expand on the techniques covered in this chapter to build more complex behaviors, such as **enemy AI, advanced pathfinding**, and **adaptive NPCs**.

Chapter 11: Multithreading and Performance Optimization

Introduction to Multithreading: Why It's Essential for Game Performance

When creating games, performance is a critical consideration. As games grow in complexity, it's essential that the game engine is capable of managing a variety of tasks simultaneously. These tasks can include handling user input, processing AI behavior, rendering graphics, and running physics simulations. Performing all of these tasks on a single processor thread can severely hinder performance, especially when your game world becomes more expansive or requires real-time responsiveness.

Multithreading offers a solution. It allows a program to execute multiple tasks simultaneously, thereby utilizing multiple CPU cores effectively. This chapter will cover the fundamentals of multithreading, its importance for game performance, common concurrency issues such as **race conditions** and **deadlocks**, and how to implement multithreading into a **game loop**.

By the end of this chapter, you will:

1. Understand the **importance of multithreading** for improving game performance.

2. Learn about **concurrency issues** such as race conditions and deadlocks, and how to address them.

3. Implement a **multithreaded game loop** for a real-time strategy (RTS) game to enhance performance.

Let's dive into how multithreading can optimize game performance and create smoother, more efficient game loops.

What You'll Need

Before we dive into multithreading concepts and the hands-on project, let's ensure you have everything needed:

Software:

- **IDE (Integrated Development Environment): Visual Studio, CLion, or Code::Blocks.** These IDEs are excellent for C++ development and support multithreading.

- **C++ Compiler**: Ensure that your IDE uses a C++ compiler with multithreading support (C++11 or later).

- **Graphics Library**: We will use **SDL2** or **SFML** for rendering and handling the window management in this project.

- **Threading Library**: The **C++ Standard Library** (<thread>) provides the tools needed for multithreading. We'll rely on this for thread management.

Hardware:

- **CPU with multiple cores**: Modern CPUs with at least **4 cores** will make multithreading more effective. This chapter is designed to work on any system with a **multicore processor**, and will perform best on **quad-core** or higher machines.

- **RAM**: **4GB of RAM** should suffice for the project, but more will be helpful for larger-scale simulations or games.

---

1. Introduction to Multithreading in Game Development

In game development, the primary goal of multithreading is to make games **responsive** and **performant**. When you run multiple tasks on different threads simultaneously, your game can handle multiple operations concurrently without waiting for one task to complete before starting another.

The Need for Multithreading in Games

Games are complex, and their **real-time nature** demands continuous updates, such as rendering, physics calculations, and AI computations. These processes need to be efficient to avoid **lag** or **frame drops**. Without multithreading, the game would be forced to process these tasks sequentially, which can lead to performance bottlenecks.

Multithreading in games can offer several benefits:

1. **Parallel Execution**: Tasks can run concurrently, improving overall performance.

2. **Responsiveness**: By dedicating separate threads to different tasks (e.g., physics simulation, AI processing), the game remains responsive to player input and other actions.

3. **Optimized Resource Utilization**: Modern CPUs have multiple cores. Multithreading allows the game to utilize all cores efficiently.

Common Multithreading Tasks in Games:

1. **Game Loop**: The main game loop that handles **rendering**, **AI**, and **physics** calculations.

2. **Physics**: Running physics simulations on a separate thread to avoid blocking the main game loop.

3. **AI**: Simulating NPC behavior in parallel with the main game flow.

4. **Networking**: Handling online multiplayer or server-client communication in the background.

---

2. Concurrency Issues: Identifying and Solving Common Problems

While multithreading improves performance, it also introduces potential **concurrency issues**. These problems arise when multiple threads interact with shared data in ways that lead to unexpected behaviors or errors. Let's explore some common issues and how to solve them.

2.1 Race Conditions

A **race condition** occurs when two or more threads attempt to read and write shared data at the same time. This can lead to inconsistent or incorrect results.

Example of a Race Condition:

Imagine two threads trying to update the **health** of an NPC in a game:

1. **Thread 1** reads the health value (let's say 100).

2. **Thread 2** reads the health value (also 100).

3. Both threads subtract 10 from the health, resulting in a final health of 90, when it should be 80.

To fix race conditions, you need to **synchronize** access to shared data between threads.

Solving Race Conditions with Mutexes:

A **mutex** (short for **mutual exclusion**) is a synchronization primitive that ensures only one thread can access the shared data at a time.

```cpp
#include <iostream>
#include <thread>
#include <mutex>

std::mutex mtx; // Mutex to protect shared resource
int health = 100;

void decreaseHealth() {
    std::lock_guard<std::mutex> lock(mtx); // Automatically locks and unlocks the mutex
    health -= 10;
}

int main() {
    std::thread t1(decreaseHealth);
    std::thread t2(decreaseHealth);

    t1.join();
    t2.join();
```

```
std::cout << "Final health: " << health << std::endl;
return 0;
}
```

In this example, the **mutex** ensures that only one thread can modify the health value at any given time, preventing the race condition.

2.2 Deadlocks

A **deadlock** occurs when two or more threads are waiting for each other to release resources, creating a situation where no thread can proceed.

Example of a Deadlock:

```
std::mutex mtx1, mtx2;

void thread1() {
    std::lock_guard<std::mutex> lock1(mtx1);
    std::this_thread::sleep_for(std::chrono::milliseconds(10)); //
Simulate some work
    std::lock_guard<std::mutex> lock2(mtx2);
}


void thread2() {
    std::lock_guard<std::mutex> lock2(mtx2);
    std::this_thread::sleep_for(std::chrono::milliseconds(10)); //
Simulate some work
    std::lock_guard<std::mutex> lock1(mtx1);
}
```

In this scenario, **thread1** locks **mtx1** and waits for **mtx2**, while **thread2** locks **mtx2** and waits for **mtx1**. This causes both threads to wait forever, creating a deadlock.

Solving Deadlocks with Lock Ordering:

To avoid deadlocks, you can **always acquire locks in the same order** to prevent circular dependencies.

---

3. Hands-On Project: Implementing a Multithreaded Game Loop

Let's put what we've learned into action by creating a **multithreaded game loop** for a **real-time strategy (RTS) game**. In this project, we will simulate game entities like **units** moving around a map while handling rendering and logic in parallel.

Step 1: Setting Up the Game Loop

In a traditional single-threaded game loop, the entire loop performs tasks such as:

- **Rendering** the game world.

- **Processing** input from the player.

- **Updating** game entities (e.g., units, buildings, etc.).

We can break these tasks into different threads to improve performance. Here's an outline of the game loop with separate threads for **input handling**, **entity movement**, and **rendering**.

Code Setup:

```
#include <iostream>
#include <thread>
```

```cpp
#include <vector>
#include <chrono>
#include <mutex>
#include <condition_variable>

// Shared resources
std::mutex mtx;
std::condition_variable cv;
bool updated = false;

struct Entity {
    int x, y;
    void move() { x++; y++; }
};

std::vector<Entity> entities;

void processInput() {
    // Simulate processing input (e.g., player commands)
    std::this_thread::sleep_for(std::chrono::milliseconds(50));
    std::lock_guard<std::mutex> lock(mtx);
    updated = true;  // Mark the game state as updated
    cv.notify_all();
}
```

```cpp
void updateEntities() {
    // Update game entities (e.g., moving units)
    std::this_thread::sleep_for(std::chrono::milliseconds(100));
    std::lock_guard<std::mutex> lock(mtx);
    if (updated) {
        for (auto& entity : entities) {
            entity.move();  // Move the entity
        }
        updated = false; // Reset flag
    }
}


void render() {
    // Render the game world (e.g., draw entities on screen)
    std::this_thread::sleep_for(std::chrono::milliseconds(200));
    std::lock_guard<std::mutex> lock(mtx);
    for (const auto& entity : entities) {
        std::cout << "Entity at: (" << entity.x << ", " << entity.y << ")\n";
    }
}


int main() {
    // Create some entities for the RTS simulation
    entities.push_back(Entity{0, 0});
    entities.push_back(Entity{5, 5});
```

```
while (true) {
    std::thread inputThread(processInput);
    std::thread updateThread(updateEntities);
    std::thread renderThread(render);

    inputThread.join();
    updateThread.join();
    renderThread.join();

    std::this_thread::sleep_for(std::chrono::milliseconds(50)); // Frame cap
}

return 0;
}
```

Step 2: Explanation

In the above example:

1. **processInput()** simulates player input handling.

2. **updateEntities()** simulates updating game entities, such as moving units.

3. **render()** renders the game world to the console.

4. The **game loop** runs continuously, creating and joining threads for each task (input, update, and render).

Multithreading Breakdown:

- **Input handling** is done on one thread, allowing the game to react to user input asynchronously.

- **Entity movement** runs on a separate thread, making sure the game world updates independently of the rendering.

- **Rendering** happens in another thread, ensuring the game state is displayed efficiently without waiting for the update logic to finish.

4. Performance Optimization

While multithreading improves the performance of the game, there are additional optimization strategies you can use:

1. **Reducing Lock Contention**: Instead of locking shared resources like the game state, use **fine-grained locks** or consider using **lock-free data structures**.

2. **Thread Pooling**: Reuse threads from a pool instead of creating and destroying threads frequently.

3. **Asynchronous Tasks**: Use **asynchronous programming** for non-blocking tasks like AI decision-making or loading assets.

Profiling and Benchmarking:

Use profiling tools (e.g., **gprof**, **Visual Studio Profiler**) to analyze where bottlenecks are happening in your game. This allows you to focus on optimizing the parts of the game that impact performance the most.

Conclusion

In this chapter, we've explored the essential concept of **multithreading** in game development, specifically:

1. The **importance of multithreading** in improving game performance and responsiveness.

2. Common **concurrency issues** like **race conditions** and **deadlocks**, and how to solve them using tools like **mutexes** and **lock guards**.

3. Implemented a **multithreaded game loop** to optimize a real-time strategy game's performance by separating tasks like **input processing**, **entity updates**, and **rendering** into different threads.

By mastering multithreading, you can create games that make full use of modern multicore processors, allowing for smoother, more dynamic gameplay. As you move forward in your game development journey, keep in mind that **performance optimization** is an ongoing process, and with multithreading, you can continually improve your game's responsiveness and efficiency.

Chapter 12: Audio and Sound Management

Introduction to Audio and Sound Management in Game Development

Sound is a powerful tool in game development, bringing the world to life through **sound effects** and **background music**. Whether it's the sound of a sword clash in a battle, the hum of a spaceship engine, or the subtle rustling of leaves in the wind, audio contributes significantly to the **atmosphere** and **immersion** of a game. But integrating sound in games goes beyond just playing sounds—it's about **managing** audio efficiently and **triggering** the right sounds at the right time in the game.

In this chapter, we will cover:

1. **Implementing sound in C++**: How to add and manage sound effects and background music in a game.

2. **Audio libraries**: Introduction to libraries like **FMOD** and **OpenAL** that provide advanced audio features.

3. **Hands-on project**: How to create a game that plays different sound effects when specific events occur, such as **collisions** or **item pickups**.

By the end of this chapter, you will have the knowledge to handle audio in your game, allowing for a richer and more engaging player experience.

What You'll Need

Before diving into the technical aspects of audio and sound management, ensure you have the following setup ready:

Software:

- **IDE (Integrated Development Environment): Visual Studio, CLion**, or **Code::Blocks**. These are perfect for C++ development.

- **C++ Compiler**: Ensure that your IDE uses a C++11 or later compiler. Visual Studio is the most common environment for audio implementation, and it works seamlessly with libraries like FMOD or OpenAL.

- **Audio Libraries**:

  o **FMOD**: A comprehensive audio library that's easy to use and provides a wide range of audio features, such as 3D sound, real-time effects, and dynamic mixing.

  o **OpenAL**: An open-source audio library that's often used in games for managing 3D spatial audio and sound effects.

- **Graphics Library**: If you're building a game with graphics, you may want to use **SFML** or **SDL2** to render and manage the game window.

- **Sound Files**: A selection of **sound effects** and **background music** in formats like **WAV** or **MP3** to use in the project.

Hardware:

- **Sound Card and Speakers/Headphones**: You'll need a working sound system to hear the audio output and test your game's sound effects.

- **Modern Computer**: A machine with at least **4GB of RAM** and a **multicore processor** is sufficient for this chapter's examples. However, complex audio tasks like spatial sound effects or streaming large music files may require a more powerful setup.

---

1. Implementing Sound in C++

C++ doesn't come with built-in audio libraries, so to add sound, we need to use external libraries that provide robust and flexible audio management. Let's start by exploring how we can integrate sound effects and background music in a C++ game.

1.1 Playing Sound Effects

To play sound effects (like gunshots, footsteps, or background sounds), you'll need an **audio library**. We'll start by using **FMOD**, a popular audio library known for its ease of use and powerful features. FMOD allows you to load audio files and play them dynamically, giving you control over volume, pitch, and playback.

Setting Up FMOD

1. **Install FMOD**:

    o   Go to the FMOD website and download the FMOD Studio API.

    o   Follow the installation instructions to link FMOD with your C++ project.

2. **Loading and Playing a Sound**: After you've set up FMOD, you can start playing sounds. Let's load a simple sound effect (e.g., a "jump" sound) and play it.

Example Code for Playing Sound:

```cpp
#include <iostream>
#include <fmod.hpp>

FMOD::System* system;
FMOD::Sound* sound;
FMOD::Channel* channel = nullptr;

void initFMOD() {
    FMOD::System_Create(&system);
    system->init(512, FMOD_INIT_NORMAL, nullptr);
}

void loadAndPlaySound(const char* filePath) {
    system->createSound(filePath, FMOD_DEFAULT, 0, &sound);
    system->playSound(sound, nullptr, false, &channel);
}

void updateAudio() {
    system->update();
}
```

```
void closeFMOD() {
    sound->release();
    system->close();
    system->release();
}

int main() {
    initFMOD();
    loadAndPlaySound("jump_sound.wav"); // Path to the sound file
    updateAudio();

    // Wait for sound to finish
    std::this_thread::sleep_for(std::chrono::seconds(2));

    closeFMOD();
    return 0;
}
```

Explanation:

- We first create an FMOD system using FMOD::System_Create() and initialize it with system->init().

- The loadAndPlaySound() function loads a sound file and plays it.

- updateAudio() ensures that FMOD keeps processing audio playback.

- Finally, we clean up resources by releasing the sound and closing the system in closeFMOD().

This code will play a sound file when executed, but this is just the beginning—FMOD gives you a lot more control over sound, including volume, pitch, looping, and 3D sound effects.

1.2 Background Music

In addition to sound effects, most games require background music. FMOD allows you to play background music in a loop or as a one-shot event. Let's extend our project to include background music.

Example Code for Background Music:

```
void playBackgroundMusic(const char* filePath) {
    FMOD::Sound* music;
    system->createSound(filePath, FMOD_LOOP_NORMAL, 0, &music);
    system->playSound(music, nullptr, false, nullptr);
}

int main() {
    initFMOD();
    playBackgroundMusic("background_music.mp3"); // Looping background music
    updateAudio();

    // Simulate game running
    std::this_thread::sleep_for(std::chrono::seconds(10));
```

```
closeFMOD();
return 0;
}
```

Explanation:

- The playBackgroundMusic() function loads the music file and sets it to **loop** using the FMOD_LOOP_NORMAL flag.

- This allows the background music to play continuously in the game.

- You can combine this with the sound effects to create a dynamic audio experience.

---

2. Audio Libraries: Using FMOD and OpenAL for Advanced Audio Features

While we've covered the basics of playing sound and background music with FMOD, let's take a look at **OpenAL**, another popular audio library, and discuss some of its advanced features.

2.1 Introduction to OpenAL

OpenAL (Open Audio Library) is an open-source, cross-platform audio library used for handling **spatial sound** (3D audio). It's widely used for games that require immersive sound environments, where sounds need to be positioned relative to the listener.

Key Features of OpenAL:

- **3D Sound**: OpenAL allows you to position sounds in a 3D space, making it ideal for games with complex sound environments (e.g., FPS or simulation games).

- **Sound Effects**: OpenAL supports various sound effects like **reverb** and **echo**.

- **Audio Sources and Listeners**: In OpenAL, you have **audio sources** (where sounds are emitted) and **listeners** (which hear the sounds).

Example Code for Playing 3D Sound in OpenAL:

```
#include <AL/al.h>
#include <AL/alc.h>

void play3DSound(const char * filePath) {
    ALuint buffer;
    ALuint source;

    // Load sound file into buffer (simplified)
    alGenBuffers(1, &buffer);
    // Normally you would load sound data here (WAV, OGG, etc.)

    // Create source for 3D sound
    alGenSources(1, &source);
    alSourcei(source, AL_BUFFER, buffer);

    // Set the position of the sound
    alSource3f(source, AL_POSITION, 0.0f, 0.0f, -5.0f); // Position 5 units away from the listener

    // Play the sound
```

```
alSourcePlay(source);

// Wait for sound to finish
std::this_thread::sleep_for(std::chrono::seconds(2));
}

int main() {
    ALCdevice * device = alcOpenDevice(nullptr);
    ALCcontext * context = alcCreateContext(device, nullptr);
    alcMakeContextCurrent(context);

    play3DSound("explosion.wav"); // Play sound at a 3D position

    alcMakeContextCurrent(nullptr);
    alcDestroyContext(context);
    alcCloseDevice(device);

    return 0;
}
```

Explanation:

- We create an **audio buffer** to store sound data (which would normally come from a file).

- An **audio source** is created to emit the sound at a specific **3D position**.

- alSource3f() sets the sound's position in the 3D space, relative to the listener's position.

OpenAL allows you to simulate environments where sounds move with respect to the player, such as the **footsteps** of enemies, **gunfire** in the distance, or **ambient sounds** like birds chirping as the player walks through a forest.

---

3. Hands-On Project: Create a Game that Plays Sound Effects on Events

Now, let's create a **game loop** that plays different sound effects when specific events occur, such as **collisions** or **item pickups**. We'll use **FMOD** to manage the sound effects and background music.

Step 1: Game Setup

We will simulate a simple game environment where the player picks up items and collides with obstacles. Each event will trigger a unique sound effect.

Code Setup:

```
#include <iostream>
#include <fmod.hpp>
#include <vector>
#include <thread>


FMOD::System* system;
FMOD::Sound* pickupSound;
FMOD::Sound* collisionSound;
```

```cpp
FMOD::Channel* channel = nullptr;

void initFMOD() {
    FMOD::System_Create(&system);
    system->init(512, FMOD_INIT_NORMAL, nullptr);
}


void loadSounds() {
    system->createSound("pickup_sound.wav", FMOD_DEFAULT,
0, &pickupSound);
    system->createSound("collision_sound.wav", FMOD_DEFAULT,
0, &collisionSound);
}


void playSound(FMOD::Sound* sound) {
    system->playSound(sound, nullptr, false, &channel);
}


void updateAudio() {
    system->update();
}


void closeFMOD() {
    pickupSound->release();
    collisionSound->release();
    system->close();
```

```cpp
    system->release();
}

int main() {
    initFMOD();
    loadSounds();

    std::cout << "Press 'P' for pickup sound or 'C' for collision sound...\n";

    char event;
    while (true) {
        std::cin >> event;
        if (event == 'P') {
            playSound(pickupSound);
        } else if (event == 'C') {
            playSound(collisionSound);
        } else {
            break;
        }

        updateAudio();
    }

    closeFMOD();
    return 0;
```

Step 2: Explanation

1. **FMOD Initialization**: We initialize FMOD and load two sound effects: **pickup_sound.wav** (for picking up items) and **collision_sound.wav** (for collisions).

2. **User Input**: We listen for the player's input. If the player presses **'P'**, the **pickup sound** is played. If the player presses **'C'**, the **collision sound** is played.

3. **Playing Sounds**: Based on the input, the corresponding sound is played by calling playSound().

4. **Looping**: The game continues to run until the user exits the loop.

This simple system simulates the behavior of a game where events trigger sound effects, enhancing the immersive experience.

Conclusion

In this chapter, we have:

1. **Implemented sound in C++** using libraries like **FMOD** and **OpenAL** to manage sound effects and background music in games.

2. Explored **advanced audio features** such as **3D sound** and **audio manipulation** with FMOD and OpenAL.

3. Created a **hands-on project** where we played sound effects based on in-game events like **collisions** and **item pickups**.

By integrating sound and music into your games, you enhance the player's immersion and emotional engagement. In future chapters, you can build upon these techniques to create more complex soundscapes, implement **interactive music systems,** or experiment with **dynamic sound effects.**

Chapter 13: Network Programming for Multiplayer Games

Introduction to Network Programming for Games

Multiplayer games are some of the most engaging and exciting experiences players can have. Whether it's a fast-paced **first-person shooter**, a strategic **real-time strategy game**, or a relaxing **co-op adventure**, multiplayer gameplay allows players to interact, collaborate, or compete in real-time over a network.

To build multiplayer games, you need to understand **network programming**—the practice of enabling computers to communicate with each other over a network. This communication involves transferring game data, synchronizing game states, and handling latency (network delay). In this chapter, we will explore how to implement network communication in games, starting with the basics of networking and progressing to more complex systems like **synchronizing game states** across players.

By the end of this chapter, you will have the knowledge to:

1. Understand the **basics of networking** and how computers communicate over a network using **TCP/IP** and **sockets**.

2. Learn how to **synchronize game states** in multiplayer games and tackle challenges like **latency** and **lag**.

3. Implement a **simple multiplayer game** (such as Pong) that demonstrates how to use networking libraries for player communication.

What You'll Need

Before we dive into the details of networking and the hands-on project, let's make sure you have the necessary tools set up.

Software:

- **IDE (Integrated Development Environment)**: Use **Visual Studio**, **CLion**, or **Code::Blocks** for C++ development.

- **C++ Compiler**: Ensure your IDE is set up with a C++11 or later compiler.

- **Networking Libraries**:

  - **Boost Asio**: A great C++ library for asynchronous networking, including support for both TCP and UDP protocols.

  - **SFML** or **SDL2**: These libraries can help with window management and graphics in the multiplayer game project.

  - Alternatively, **Winsock** (Windows) or **Berkeley Sockets** (Linux/macOS) can be used directly for socket programming.

Hardware:

- A computer with **internet access** for the multiplayer game project, so you can test the network communication.

- **Two computers** (optional but recommended) for testing the game across different machines. If using a single computer, you can test the server and client on different processes.

1. Basics of Networking: Introduction to TCP/IP, Sockets, and Communication

In networking, the goal is to allow two or more computers to communicate over the internet or local network. This is achieved by using **protocols**—rules and formats for communication.

1.1 TCP/IP Protocols

The **TCP/IP** (Transmission Control Protocol/Internet Protocol) suite is the foundation of modern internet communication. It defines how data should be **packaged**, **addressed**, and **transmitted** between computers over a network.

- **TCP (Transmission Control Protocol)**: A reliable, connection-oriented protocol that ensures data is delivered in the correct order and without errors. TCP is often used for applications where data integrity is crucial, such as file transfers, web browsing, and multiplayer games.

- **UDP (User Datagram Protocol)**: A connectionless, less reliable protocol that is faster than TCP. UDP is often used for real-time applications like gaming, where speed is more important than perfect accuracy (e.g., **real-time strategy games** or **FPS**).

For multiplayer games, **TCP** is typically used for critical data like player authentication, while **UDP** is used for real-time game state updates, where small packet losses are acceptable.

1.2 Sockets

A **socket** is an endpoint for sending or receiving data across a network. In the context of game development, sockets are used to establish communication between the **client** (player's computer) and the **server** (the host or game server).

- **Client:** The player's machine or application that connects to a server and sends/receives game data.

- **Server:** The machine that hosts the game and listens for incoming client connections.

Creating a Basic Socket

In C++, sockets are typically managed using **Berkeley Sockets** (for Unix/Linux) or **Winsock** (for Windows). Here's an example of how to create a basic TCP socket in C++ using **Boost Asio:**

```cpp
#include <boost/asio.hpp>
#include <iostream>

using namespace boost::asio;
using ip::tcp;

int main() {
    io_service io_service;

    // Create a TCP socket and connect to the server
    tcp::socket socket(io_service);
    socket.connect(tcp::endpoint(ip::address::from_string("127.0.0.1"), 8080)); // Local server, port 8080
```

```
// Send a message to the server
std::string message = "Hello from client!";
socket.send(buffer(message));

// Close the socket
socket.close();

std::cout << "Message sent to server." << std::endl;
return 0;
}
```

In this example:

- We use **Boost Asio** to create a socket, connect it to a local server at **127.0.0.1** on port **8080**, and send a message.

- The **buffer()** function is used to convert the message string into a format that can be sent over the network.

2. Multiplayer Games: Synchronizing Game States and Handling Latency

In multiplayer games, synchronization of game states across multiple players is crucial. The game world must remain consistent for all players, even though they are on different machines.

2.1 Synchronizing Game States

In real-time multiplayer games, **game state synchronization** means that actions performed by players (e.g., moving, shooting, or picking up items) need to be reflected in real-time on all players' machines.

Common synchronization techniques:

- **Polling**: Clients frequently send updates to the server, which then broadcasts these updates to other clients.

- **Event-based**: Events (like a player's action) are sent to the server, and the server broadcasts relevant events to all connected clients.

- **Prediction and Correction**: The client predicts the result of an action (e.g., movement), and the server sends corrections if the prediction is wrong.

2.2 Handling Latency

Latency (network delay) is one of the biggest challenges in multiplayer games. It's the time it takes for data to travel from the client to the server and back. High latency can cause **lag**, where players' actions are delayed, resulting in poor gameplay experiences.

Here are some strategies for handling latency:

- **Lag Compensation**: The server can account for player latency and adjust the game state accordingly. For example, if a player shoots a gun, the server might predict where the shot will land based on the player's latency.

- **Client-Side Prediction**: The client can predict the outcome of its actions (e.g., moving or shooting) to reduce the appearance of lag. If the server's response is different, the client adjusts.

- **Server Reconciliation**: The server periodically sends the **authoritative state** of the game, and clients reconcile their states with the server's state.

2.3 Bandwidth Management

Sending too much data over the network can overwhelm the available bandwidth, especially in games with a lot of real-time actions. It's essential to minimize the amount of data sent by:

- **Sending updates only when the game state changes** (e.g., when a player moves or performs an action).

- **Compressing data**: Sending smaller packets can reduce the load on the network.

---

3. Hands-On Project: Building a Simple Multiplayer Game Using Networking Libraries

Now that we understand the basics of networking, game state synchronization, and latency handling, let's build a **simple multiplayer game**—a basic **Pong** game—using **Boost Asio** for networking.

Step 1: Game Design Overview

The Pong game will involve two players: one on the **left** side and one on the **right** side. Players control paddles and try to bounce the ball past their opponent. We will use **TCP** sockets to communicate between the server and clients.

- The **server** will handle the game logic and maintain the game state (ball position, paddle positions).

- The **clients** will display the game state and send input (e.g., paddle movement) to the server.

Step 2: Setting Up the Server

The server will handle the game logic and synchronize the game state with the connected clients.

```cpp
#include <boost/asio.hpp>
#include <iostream>
#include <thread>
#include <vector>

using boost::asio::ip::tcp;

struct GameState {
    int ballX, ballY, paddleLeftY, paddleRightY;
};

class GameServer {
public:
    GameServer(boost::asio::io_service& io_service, short port)
        : acceptor_(io_service, tcp::endpoint(tcp::v4(), port)) {
        startAccept();
    }

    void startAccept() {
        tcp::socket socket(io_service_);
        acceptor_.async_accept(socket,
            [this, &socket](const boost::system::error_code& error) {
```

```cpp
        if (!error) {
            startGame(std::move(socket));
        }
        startAccept();
    });
}


void startGame(tcp::socket socket) {
    GameState gameState = { 50, 50, 30, 30 }; // Initial ball and
paddle positions
    std::vector<tcp::socket> clients = { std::move(socket) };

    while (true) {
        // Game loop: update game state and send it to clients
        gameState.ballX += 1; // Simple ball movement for
demonstration

        // Send game state to all connected clients
        for (auto& client : clients) {
            boost::asio::write(client, boost::asio::buffer(&gameState,
sizeof(gameState)));
        }

        // Simulate game logic (e.g., ball bouncing, paddle collision)
        std::this_thread::sleep_for(std::chrono::milliseconds(16)); //
60 FPS
    }
```

```
    }


private:

    boost::asio::io_service io_service_;

    tcp::acceptor acceptor_;

};
```

Step 3: Setting Up the Client

The client will display the game and send player input (e.g., paddle movement) to the server.

```
#include <boost/asio.hpp>
#include <iostream>


using boost::asio::ip::tcp;


struct GameState {
    int ballX, ballY, paddleLeftY, paddleRightY;
};


class GameClient {
public:
    GameClient(boost::asio::io_service& io_service, const std::string& host, short port)
        : socket_(io_service) {
        connect(host, port);
    }
```

```cpp
    void connect(const std::string& host, short port) {
        tcp::resolver resolver(io_service_);
        tcp::resolver::query query(host, std::to_string(port));
        tcp::resolver::iterator endpoint_iterator =
resolver.resolve(query);
        boost::asio::connect(socket_, endpoint_iterator);
    }


    void receiveGameState() {
        GameState gameState;
        while (true) {
            boost::asio::read(socket_, boost::asio::buffer(&gameState,
sizeof(gameState)));
            std::cout << "Ball Position: (" << gameState.ballX << ", " <<
gameState.ballY << ")\n";
        }
    }

private:
    boost::asio::io_service io_service_;
    tcp::socket socket_;
};

int main() {
    boost::asio::io_service io_service;
    GameClient client(io_service, "127.0.0.1", 8080); // Connect to
server
```

client.receiveGameState();

return 0;

}

Step 4: Running the Multiplayer Game

To run the multiplayer game, compile the server and client programs separately. Start the server first, then connect multiple clients to it.

Conclusion

In this chapter, we have:

1. Explored the basics of **network programming** for multiplayer games, focusing on **TCP/IP** and **sockets**.

2. Learned about **game state synchronization**, **latency handling**, and strategies for **bandwidth management** in multiplayer games.

3. Implemented a **multiplayer Pong game** using **Boost Asio** for network communication, allowing two clients to play the game over the network.

Multiplayer game development introduces new challenges and exciting opportunities for creating engaging player experiences. As you continue to build on these concepts, you can extend this knowledge to create more complex multiplayer games, handle larger player counts, and implement **real-time features** like **chat systems**, **matchmaking**, and **lobbies**.

Chapter 14: Testing and Debugging C++ Games

Introduction: The Importance of Testing and Debugging in Game Development

Creating games is a complex and intricate process, and as your game grows in size and complexity, so do the potential for **bugs**, **crashes**, and **performance issues**. One of the most crucial parts of development is **testing** and **debugging**. It's not just about finding and fixing issues; it's about ensuring that your game runs **smoothly**, is **robust**, and delivers a **polished experience** to the player.

In this chapter, we'll delve into the world of **debugging tools**, **unit testing**, and how to **test game features** to ensure they are functioning as expected. By the end of this chapter, you'll have a solid understanding of how to:

1. Use **debugging tools** like **GDB**, **Valgrind**, and **IDE debuggers** to troubleshoot and resolve issues.

2. Implement **unit testing** using frameworks like **Google Test** to validate game code functionality.

3. Develop practical skills by debugging and testing a game feature using unit tests to ensure robustness.

What You'll Need

To follow along with this chapter, ensure you have the following tools and software:

Software:

- **C++ Development Environment: Visual Studio, Code::Blocks**, or **CLion**. These IDEs will support you with debugging tools and unit testing framework integration.

- **Debugging Tools:**

    o **GDB**: The GNU Debugger, a powerful debugging tool for analyzing and troubleshooting C++ applications.

    o **Valgrind**: A tool for memory management debugging and detecting memory leaks and errors.

    o **IDE Debugger**: Most modern IDEs come with integrated debuggers that can help you step through your code.

- **Unit Testing Framework:**

    o **Google Test**: A widely used unit testing framework for C++. It helps ensure that individual components of your game function as expected.

- **Game Development Tools**: You'll need a basic game engine setup, whether it's using **SFML, SDL2**, or a custom game engine.

Hardware:

- A **modern laptop or desktop** with **4GB RAM** or more is sufficient for this chapter. Debugging tools can sometimes use significant resources, so ensure your system is relatively powerful.

- **Debugger Support**: Ensure your computer supports GDB or the integrated debugger in your IDE for efficient debugging.

1. Debugging Tools: Introduction to Debugging in Game Development

Debugging is a critical skill in game development. Games often have complex logic, interactions, and performance requirements that can make finding bugs a challenge. Fortunately, various debugging tools are available to help you track down issues.

1.1 GDB (GNU Debugger)

GDB is a powerful command-line debugger for C++ and many other languages. It helps developers inspect the state of their program while it's running, examine the call stack, and pinpoint exactly where things go wrong. It's especially useful when your game crashes, or you need to understand why certain behaviors are happening in your game.

Key GDB Features:

- **Breakpoints**: Stop execution at a specific point in your code.

- **Step-by-Step Execution**: Run the code line-by-line to observe how the program executes.

- **Variable Inspection**: Examine the values of variables at different points in the program.

- **Call Stack Trace**: See the functions that have been called leading up to an issue.

Basic GDB Workflow:

Compile your program with debug information:

g++ -g mygame.cpp -o mygame

Start GDB:

gdb ./mygame

Set a breakpoint at a function or line number:

break main

Run the program inside GDB:

run

Step through the program, examine variables, and check the call stack:

next // Execute the next line

print variable_name // Print the value of a variable

backtrace // Display the call stack

1.2 Valgrind: Memory Management Debugging

Valgrind is a tool that helps you find memory-related errors in your program, such as memory leaks, invalid memory accesses, and memory corruption. It's particularly helpful in C++ because the language doesn't have garbage collection, which increases the potential for memory management issues.

Common Valgrind Use Cases:

- **Memory Leaks**: When memory is allocated but not freed.

- **Invalid Memory Access**: When the program reads or writes to unallocated or freed memory.

Running Valgrind:

valgrind --leak-check=full ./mygame

This will run your game while checking for memory issues. Valgrind will output any detected memory leaks or errors in your code, and you can fix them to improve the game's stability and performance.

1.3 IDE Debuggers

Most modern **Integrated Development Environments (IDEs)**, like **Visual Studio** or **CLion**, come with **built-in debuggers** that offer graphical user interfaces for debugging. These debuggers often provide the same functionality as GDB but with a more user-friendly interface.

Key features include:

- **Breakpoints**: Set breakpoints by clicking on the line number.

- **Watch Variables**: Track the value of variables as you step through your code.

- **Call Stack**: View the call stack and navigate to previous function calls.

- **Step-by-Step Debugging**: Execute your code one line at a time, watching variable changes and program flow.

---

2. Unit Testing in C++

In addition to debugging, **unit testing** is an essential part of maintaining robust and reliable game code. Unit testing allows you to write **automated tests** to verify that specific components of your game work correctly. By using **unit testing frameworks** like **Google Test**, you can ensure that bugs are caught early and your game remains stable as you add new features.

2.1 Introduction to Unit Testing

Unit testing involves writing tests for **individual units** of your program, such as functions, classes, or modules. In C++, unit tests are typically written in **test functions** that assert specific outcomes, like whether a function returns the expected value or whether an object is in the correct state.

Benefits of Unit Testing:

- **Early Bug Detection**: Catch errors before they become issues in production.

- **Refactoring Support**: Refactor your code with confidence, knowing that your tests will catch any regressions.

- **Code Quality**: Writing tests encourages you to write cleaner, more modular code.

2.2 Setting Up Google Test in C++

Google Test is a powerful and widely-used unit testing framework for C++. It allows you to write tests and assertions in a structured way.

Steps to Install Google Test:

1. Download Google Test from GitHub.

2. Follow the installation instructions to set up Google Test in your project.

Writing a Simple Unit Test Using Google Test:

Here's an example of a simple unit test using Google Test to test a function that adds two numbers:

```cpp
#include <gtest/gtest.h>

// Function to be tested
int add(int a, int b) {
    return a + b;
}
```

```
// Unit test for add() function
TEST(AddTest, PositiveNumbers) {
    EXPECT_EQ(add(2, 3), 5);  // Test that 2 + 3 equals 5
}


TEST(AddTest, NegativeNumbers) {
    EXPECT_EQ(add(-1, -1), -2);  // Test that -1 + -1 equals -2
}


int main(int argc, char** argv) {
    ::testing::InitGoogleTest(&argc, argv);
    return RUN_ALL_TESTS();
}
```

Running the Unit Tests:

1. Build your project with Google Test linked.

2. Run your tests:

3. ./mygame_tests

If any of the assertions fail, Google Test will output an error message showing which test failed and why.

2.3 Advanced Unit Testing Techniques

- **Mocking**: Sometimes, you need to mock dependencies to isolate the unit being tested. For example, mocking a database or network connection in unit tests.

- **Parameterized Tests**: These allow you to run the same test with different inputs, improving test coverage.

- **Test Suites**: Group multiple related tests into suites to organize tests by functionality.

---

3. Hands-On Project: Debug and Test a Game Feature

In this project, we will implement a feature in a simple game, debug it using GDB and Valgrind, and then write unit tests to ensure robustness. Let's simulate a **simple health system** for a game character.

Step 1: Implement the Health System

We will implement a class called Character that has a **health attribute**. The character will be able to **take damage** and **heal**. We'll implement basic functions for this and include logic to check for health overflow or underflow.

```
class Character {
public:
    Character(int maxHealth) : health(maxHealth),
maxHealth(maxHealth) {}


    void takeDamage(int damage) {
        health -= damage;
        if (health < 0) health = 0;  // Prevent health from going below 0
    }
```

```cpp
void heal(int healingAmount) {
    health += healingAmount;
    if (health > maxHealth) health = maxHealth; // Prevent health
from exceeding maxHealth
  }

  int getHealth() const { return health; }

private:
    int health;
    int maxHealth;
};
```

Step 2: Write Unit Tests for the Health System

Now, we'll write unit tests to ensure that the health system works correctly. We'll test that the character's health cannot go below zero or exceed the maximum.

```cpp
#include <gtest/gtest.h>

TEST(CharacterTest, TakeDamage) {
    Character character(100);
    character.takeDamage(30);
    EXPECT_EQ(character.getHealth(), 70);

    character.takeDamage(100); // Taking more damage than current
health
    EXPECT_EQ(character.getHealth(), 0); // Health should be 0
```

```
}

TEST(CharacterTest, Heal) {
    Character character(100);
    character.takeDamage(50);
    character.heal(30);
    EXPECT_EQ(character.getHealth(), 80);

    character.heal(50);  // Healing more than maxHealth
    EXPECT_EQ(character.getHealth(), 100);  // Health should be
capped at maxHealth
}

int main(int argc, char **argv) {
    ::testing::InitGoogleTest(&argc, argv);
    return RUN_ALL_TESTS();
}
```

Step 3: Debugging with GDB and Valgrind

1. **GDB:** Use GDB to step through the code and watch how the health system behaves during execution. Set breakpoints in the takeDamage and heal functions to inspect the health variable.

2. gdb ./mygame

3. break takeDamage

4. run

5. **Valgrind**: Run the program with Valgrind to check for memory leaks or memory access violations.

6. valgrind --leak-check=full ./mygame

Step 4: Running the Unit Tests

Finally, compile and run the unit tests to verify that the health system behaves as expected. If all tests pass, you can be confident that the feature is robust.

Conclusion

In this chapter, we've covered:

1. The **importance of debugging** and **unit testing** in game development to ensure robust, error-free code.

2. How to use debugging tools like **GDB**, **Valgrind**, and **IDE debuggers** to troubleshoot and optimize your game.

3. The process of writing **unit tests** using **Google Test**, allowing you to validate that your game logic functions correctly.

4. A hands-on project where we implemented and tested a simple **health system** for a game character.

Testing and debugging are essential skills that every game developer must master. They ensure that your game is **reliable**, **efficient**, and ready for release. By incorporating **automated testing** into your development workflow, you can catch bugs early, refactor with confidence, and provide a better experience for your players.

Chapter 15: Building, Deploying, and Optimizing Final Projects

Introduction: Preparing Your Game for Launch

After months of development, testing, and debugging, your game is almost ready for players. However, before you can share your creation with the world, you must prepare it for **distribution**, ensure it performs well across different platforms, and implement the final **optimizations** for smooth performance.

In this chapter, we'll explore how to:

1. **Package your game** for different platforms (Windows, macOS, and consoles).

2. Apply **final optimization techniques** to ensure your game runs smoothly, even under heavy load.

3. **Deploy your game** and get it ready for distribution on platforms like Steam, the **Epic Games Store**, or even consoles.

4. Implement a **build pipeline** to automate the building, testing, and deployment of your game.

By the end of this chapter, you'll have the tools to finalize your game, optimize its performance, and get it ready for launch on multiple platforms.

What You'll Need

Before diving into the process of packaging, optimizing, and deploying your game, let's ensure you have the right tools in place:

Software:

- **Game Engine or Framework**: Use **SFML**, **SDL2**, or a custom game engine. If you're using a third-party game engine like **Unity** or **Unreal Engine**, they have built-in tools for packaging and deployment.

- **Build System**: A **build automation system** like **CMake** or **Makefile** will help manage the compilation process, ensuring that everything is properly built for distribution.

- **Platform-Specific SDKs**: For targeting specific platforms like **Windows, macOS**, or **consoles**, you may need the respective **SDKs** (Software Development Kits) installed.

  - For **Windows**, you can use **MSVC** (Microsoft Visual C++).

  - For **macOS**, you'll need **Xcode** installed.

  - For **consoles**, you'll need specific development kits like **PlayStation SDK** or **Xbox Development Kit**.

- **Graphics and Audio Tools**: If you're optimizing textures, audio, or other assets, tools like **Photoshop**, **Audacity**, or **Blender** will be necessary for final tweaks.

- **Version Control**: Use **Git** and services like **GitHub** or **GitLab** for collaboration and managing your game's codebase.

Hardware:

- A **modern computer** (laptop or desktop) with at least **8GB RAM** (16GB recommended for large projects).

- **Graphics Card (GPU)**: Ensure your machine has a **dedicated GPU** if you're optimizing GPU performance or testing graphical elements.

- **Multiple Devices**: For cross-platform deployment, it's helpful to test your game on different machines, including **Windows** and **macOS**, or even a **console** if targeting one.

1. Packaging Your Game for Distribution

Before your game can be distributed, it needs to be **packaged** in a way that's easy for players to download and run. Packaging involves preparing the game files, including the executable, assets, and any necessary dependencies, for each platform you want to support.

1.1 Packaging for Windows

Windows is the most common platform for games, and packaging your game for Windows typically involves the following steps:

Creating the Executable:

1. **Build your game** into an executable file using your IDE. For example, in **Visual Studio**, this is usually done by building the project in **Release mode** to create an optimized executable.

2. **Include the necessary dependencies** (e.g., DLL files for libraries like **FMOD** or **SDL2**). You can statically link libraries, but it's often easier to distribute the **DLLs** alongside the executable.

Creating the Installer:

For ease of installation, you may want to create an installer for your game. You can use tools like:

- **Inno Setup**: A free tool that allows you to create simple and professional Windows installers.

- **NSIS (Nullsoft Scriptable Install System)**: Another free tool for creating Windows installers, particularly useful for larger games.

Example: Simple Inno Setup Script:

[Setup]
AppName=MyGame
AppVersion=1.0
DefaultDirName={pf}\MyGame
DefaultGroupName=MyGame
OutputDir=.\Output
OutputBaseFilename=MyGameSetup
Compression=lzma
SolidCompression=yes

[Files]
Source: "bin\Release\mygame.exe"; DestDir: "{app}"; Flags: ignoreversion
*Source: "bin\Release\ *.dll"; DestDir: "{app}"; Flags: ignoreversion*

This script will package your executable and DLLs into an installer.

1.2 Packaging for macOS

Packaging a game for macOS requires a slightly different approach. macOS applications are typically packaged into an **.app** bundle, which contains the executable, assets, and all dependencies. Here's a general outline of the process:

Creating the Executable:

1. **Build the game** using **Xcode** or **CMake**. For C++ projects, you can use CMake to generate Xcode project files.

2. **Code-signing**: Apple requires that applications be signed with a developer certificate to avoid warnings when players try to launch the game. Use **Xcode** or **Apple Developer tools** to sign your game.

Creating the .app Bundle:

You can use **Xcode** to package the game into a macOS app bundle, or manually create the structure:

- MyGame.app/Contents/MacOS/: Place the executable here.

- MyGame.app/Contents/Resources/: Store game assets like images, sounds, and configuration files.

Distributing via the Mac App Store:

To distribute your game on the **Mac App Store**, you must adhere to Apple's guidelines and submit the game through **Xcode** and the **Apple Developer Portal**.

1.3 Packaging for Consoles

Deploying games to consoles like **PlayStation**, **Xbox**, or **Nintendo Switch** requires specific **SDKs** and developer access to the respective platforms. These tools provide unique features for packaging games for consoles.

- **PlayStation** and **Xbox** both provide their own **development kits** (PS SDK and Xbox DevKit), and the process involves creating the console-specific executable and assets before submitting the game to the respective console store.

- **Nintendo Switch**: Requires integration with the **Nintendo Switch SDK**, which includes tools for managing game packaging, testing, and submission.

For these platforms, you'll need to be a registered developer with access to the SDKs and the platform's submission process.

---

2. Optimization Techniques: Final Optimizations for CPU and GPU

Now that your game is ready for distribution, it's time to focus on optimizing its performance to ensure it runs smoothly on various systems. Game optimization is crucial for providing a **seamless** experience for players, especially on lower-end devices or machines with limited resources.

2.1 CPU Optimization

CPU optimization ensures that the game logic runs as efficiently as possible, without overloading the CPU and causing performance bottlenecks.

1. Efficient Algorithms:

Ensure that the algorithms you use are optimized for performance. For example:

- Use **O(n)** or better algorithms for tasks like pathfinding, searching, and sorting.

- Avoid using **nested loops** for operations that need to be performed on large datasets.

2. Multithreading:

By using **multithreading** (discussed in Chapter 11), you can split heavy tasks like AI processing, physics calculations, and game logic across multiple CPU cores, making your game run faster on multi-core systems.

3. Avoiding Unnecessary Memory Allocations:

Frequent memory allocations and deallocations can cause performance hits due to **memory fragmentation**. Use **memory pools** and **object recycling** to reduce the number of allocations.

2.2 GPU Optimization

The **GPU** is responsible for rendering the visuals in your game, and optimizing it is crucial for improving the frame rate and reducing graphical glitches.

1. Reducing Draw Calls:

Each time the GPU renders an object, it needs to make a **draw call**. Too many draw calls can significantly slow down the game, especially for complex scenes. To reduce draw calls:

- **Batch render** multiple objects using the same texture.

- Use **instancing** to draw multiple copies of the same object with a single call.

2. Optimizing Shaders:

Shaders are often the most performance-intensive part of the graphics pipeline. You can optimize shaders by:

- Avoiding unnecessary calculations inside shaders (e.g., use precomputed values where possible).

- Using **simpler shaders** for objects that are far from the camera or don't require high levels of detail.

3. Level of Detail (LOD):

For distant objects, use lower-quality models (lower polygon count) to reduce the GPU's workload. This technique is known as **Level of Detail (LOD)**, and it helps maintain frame rates while still displaying visually appealing objects.

4. Texture Optimization:

Textures consume a significant amount of GPU memory. You can reduce texture memory usage by:

- Compressing textures.

- Using **mipmaps** to store smaller versions of textures for distant objects.

3. Deployment: Preparing Your Game for Deployment

Once your game is packaged and optimized, you need to prepare it for deployment. Deployment involves distributing your game to the platform where players can download and install it.

3.1 Preparing for Deployment on Windows

For **Windows**, deployment typically involves:

1. **Creating an installer** (as discussed earlier in the chapter).

2. **Testing the game on different hardware** configurations to ensure it runs smoothly on low, mid, and high-end systems.

3. **Distributing via platforms like Steam or the Microsoft Store**.

3.2 Preparing for Deployment on macOS

For **macOS**, follow the steps mentioned earlier to package your game into an **.app bundle**. If distributing via the **Mac App Store**, ensure your game adheres to Apple's guidelines and use **Xcode** to submit it.

3.3 Preparing for Deployment on Consoles

Deploying on **PlayStation**, **Xbox**, or **Nintendo Switch** requires submitting your game to the respective **game stores** after following their submission process. This involves:

- Creating console-specific builds.

- Code-signing your game for security.

- Testing with the console's **development kits** to ensure everything functions as expected.

4. Hands-On Project: Creating a Build Pipeline for Your Game

In this project, we will create a **build pipeline** for your game, ensuring that it's optimized and ready for launch. We'll automate the build process, handle testing, and ensure that everything is ready for deployment.

Step 1: Set Up a CMake Build System

Create a **CMakeLists.txt** file that handles your build process. This will ensure your game is compiled correctly for multiple platforms.

```
cmake_minimum_required(VERSION 3.10)


project(MyGame)


set(CMAKE_CXX_STANDARD 11)


# Add source files
add_executable(MyGame main.cpp game.cpp)


# Link libraries
target_link_libraries(MyGame sfml-graphics sfml-window sfml-system)
```

Step 2: Automate Testing

Use **Google Test** to write and automate unit tests as part of the build process. You can configure **CMake** to run tests during the build:

```
enable_testing()
add_subdirectory(tests)
```

Step 3: Deploying and Packaging

For packaging, automate the creation of installers (on Windows) or app bundles (on macOS) using **Inno Setup** (Windows) or **App Bundler** (macOS).

Conclusion

In this chapter, we've covered the essential steps for getting your game ready for launch:

1. **Packaging your game** for distribution on platforms like **Windows, macOS**, and **consoles**.

2. **Optimizing your game** for CPU and GPU performance to ensure a smooth experience for players.

3. **Deploying your game** and preparing it for submission to stores like **Steam** or the **Mac App Store**.

4. We completed a **hands-on project** where we created a build pipeline, ensuring our game is properly built, tested, and ready for launch.

By following these steps, you'll ensure that your game is not only optimized for performance but also packaged and ready for deployment on various platforms, ensuring the best possible experience for your players.